PROFILES IN MATHEMATICS

Alan Turing

Profiles in Mathematics:
Alan Turing

Jim Corrigan

MORGAN REYNOLDS
PUBLISHING
Greensboro, North Carolina

Profiles in Mathematics:

Alan Turing

Rene' Descartes

Carl Friedrich Gauss

Sophie Germain

Pierre de Fermat

Ancient Mathematicians

Women Mathematicians

PROFILES IN MATHEMATICS
ALAN TURING

Copyright © 2009 By Jim Corrigan

Library of Congress Cataloging-in-Publication Data

Corrigan, Jim.
  Alan Turing / by Jim Corrigan.
    p. cm. -- (Profiles in mathematics)
  Includes bibliographical references and index.
  ISBN-13: 978-1-59935-064-6
  ISBN-10: 1-59935-064-5
  1. Turing, Alan Mathison, 1912-1954. 2. Mathematicians--Great Britain-
-Biography. I. Title.
  QA29.T8C67 2007
  510.92--dc22
  [B]

                                                    2007011704

Printed in the United States of America
First Edition

For my wife, Connie, with love

Contents

Introduction 10

Chapter One
Early Discoveries 13

Chapter Two
Universal Turing Machine 24

Chapter Three
Unraveling the Enigma 37

Chapter Four
Beyond Bletchley Park 51

Chapter Five
Building a Brain 61

Chapter Six
Mathematical Biology 74

Chapter Seven
Poison Apple 85

Chapter Eight
Alan Turing's Legacy 95

Timeline 105
Sources 107
Bibliography 109
Web sites 110
Index 111

Introduction

Mathematics gives us a powerful way to analyze and try to understand many of the things we observe around us, from the spread of epidemics and the orbit of planets, to grade point averages and the distance between cities. Mathematics also has been used to search for spiritual truth, as well as the more abstract question of what is knowledge itself.

Perhaps the most intriguing question about mathematics is where does it come from? Is it discovered, or is it invented? Does nature order the world by mathematical principles, and the mathematician's job is to uncover this underlying system? Or is mathematics created by mathematicians as developing cultures and technologies require it? This unanswerable question has intrigued mathematicians and scientists for thousands of years and is at the heart of this new series of biographies.

The development of mathematical knowledge has progressed, in fits and starts, for thousands of years. People from various areas and cultures have discovered new mathematical concepts and devised complex systems of algorithms and equations that have both practical and philosophical impact.

To learn more of the history of mathematics is to encounter some of the greatest minds in human history. Regardless of whether they were discoverers or inventors, these fascinating lives are filled with countless memorable stories—stories filled with the same tragedy, triumph, and persistence of genius as that of the world's great writers, artists, and musicians.

Knowledge of Pythagoras, René Descartes, Carl Friedrich Gauss, Sophie Germain, Alan Turing, and others will help to lift mathematics off the page and out of the calculator, and into the minds and imaginations of readers. As mathematics becomes more and more ingrained in our day-to-day lives, awakening students to its history becomes especially important.

Sharon F. Doorasamy
Editor in chief

Editorial Consultant

In his youth, Curt Gabrielson was inspired by reading the biographies of dozens of great mathematicians and scientists. "I was driven to learn math when I was young, because math is the language of physical science," says Curt, who named his dog Archimedes. "I now know also that it stands alone, beautiful and mysterious." He learned the more practical side of mathematics growing up on his family's hog farm in Missouri, designing and building structures, fixing electrical systems and machines, and planning for the yearly crops.

After earning a BS in physics from MIT and working at the San Francisco Exploratorium for several years, Curt spent two years in China teaching English, science, and math, and two years in Timor-Leste, one of the world's newest democracies, helping to create the first physics department at the country's National University, as well as a national teacher-training program. In 1997, he spearheaded the Watsonville Science Workshop in northern California, which has earned him recognition from the U.S. Congress, the California State Assembly, and the national Association of Mexican American educators. Mathematics instruction at the Workshop includes games, puzzles, geometric construction, and abacuses.

Curt Gabrielson is the author of several journal articles, as well as the book *Stomp Rockets, Catapults, and Kaleidoscopes: 30+Amazing Science Projects You Can Build for Less than $1.*

Alan Turing *(Courtesy of King's College Library, Cambridge)*

one
Early
Discoveries

I n early May 1926, Great Britain's coal miners went on
strike. Many other workers also left their jobs in a show
of support, quickly causing great disruption throughout
the country. The labor strike posed something of a problem
for thirteen-year-old Alan Turing. He was set to arrive at his
new boarding school for the start of the summer term, but
now the trains were not running and the school was more
than sixty miles away.

Alan was nothing if not independent and resourceful.
Bicycling was still a common form of transportation, and
he calculated that he could cycle the sixty-mile distance in
about two days. Amid striking workers, Alan set out on his
solitary journey across the English countryside. At the end of
the first day, he arranged overnight lodging for himself and
wrote home with an update on his progress. The second leg

of his trip went smoothly as well, and soon he was pedaling up the boulevard to his school.

The story of the youth's impromptu bicycle trek attracted much attention, even inspiring an article in the local newspaper. Many adults found it extraordinary that an adolescent could show such initiative and self-reliance. But to Alan, there was nothing extraordinary about it at all. He had merely devised a practical solution to an everyday problem, and then executed it. That no-nonsense attitude was something he would carry with him throughout his entire life. Turing was never interested in prestige or recognition; in fact, he avoided the limelight. He simply wanted to find answers.

The bicycle episode revealed another defining element of Alan Turing's personality: he preferred to work alone. In the years ahead, as his remarkable intellectual powers slowly became apparent, it became equally apparent that he would not adhere to the norms of society. His disheveled appearance, his halting manner of speaking, and his multitude of peculiar habits tended to isolate him from the rest of the world. Even his small circle of friends never fully understood him. To most people, he seemed the classic absent-minded professor: an unapproachable genius, so distracted by his latest brilliant theory that

Alan's mother, Sara *(Courtesy of King's College Library, Cambridge)*

he failed to notice the missing buttons and frayed edges on his threadbare clothes.

Alan Mathison Turing was the second child of Julius Turing and Ethel Sara Stoney Turing. The couple met aboard a ship returning to England from India, which was a British colony at the time. Julius had been working as a government administrator in India, while Sara, as she preferred to be called, was staying there with her fam-

Alan's father, Julius *(Courtesy of King's College Library, Cambridge)*

ily. They married in the fall of 1907, and their first son, John, was born a year later. Alan, the last child, arrived on June 23, 1912.

Julius Turing's work required that he and his wife return to India for extended periods, but they wanted their sons to grow up in England. John and Alan spent much of their childhood in the homes of family friends or at boarding school. This arrangement no doubt contributed to Alan's sense of self-sufficiency. He taught himself to read in three weeks before he was old enough to attend school, but it was clear he preferred numbers to words. He was fascinated by numbers, going so far as to take note of lamppost serial numbers while walking down the street.

Alan Turing was not a perfect student, however. Headmasters routinely complained about his sloppy penmanship, his lack of organization, and his inattention to detail. Instead of focusing on his schoolwork, they complained, Alan always seemed to be thinking about something else. He spent his free time studying—but only the subjects he found interesting, not what his teachers thought he should learn. While his classmates might be memorizing Latin phrases, Alan would be busy examining a map of Britain, or a recipe he found in an old book.

He seemed interested in any topic that involved the application of logic. Chess was a particular favorite, although his skill at the game never rose far above average. He was thrilled when the use of logic had a practical result. For example, while enjoying a summer picnic in 1919,

A young Alan poses for a photo in 1917. *(Courtesy of King's College Library, Cambridge)*

he amazed his family by suddenly producing fresh honey for their tea. He had carefully observed the flight patterns of wild bees in a nearby field, and then used those patterns to extrapolate the location of their hive.

Alan was deeply intrigued by nature. At age ten, he received a gift that helped shape his view of the world—a book entitled

Natural Wonders Every Child Should Know, by the American author Edwin Tenney Brewster. The volume was an introduction to science, with a particular emphasis on biology. It provided basic answers to the questions children instinctively ask, such as how they came to be, and how the human body works. Brewster compared the body to a machine, noting that both must take in fuel and convert it to energy in order to perform tasks. He explained that children must go to school so that their brains can learn to perform the necessary tasks in life. Alan Turing never forgot the simple analogy. Many of his future achievements would come from thinking of the human brain as a machine—and from thinking about how a machine might function like the human brain.

Alan's investigation of the natural world led him to chemistry. When he was twelve his parents gave him a chemistry set for Christmas, but Mr. and Mrs. Turing were somewhat puzzled by their younger son's strange hobbies. Scientific endeavors were not held in very high esteem in British culture of the 1920s. They wished that Alan would instead turn his attention to languages, writing, and sports. These were the subjects that would get him ahead in school, and perhaps win him a scholarship. But it was not to be. Alan continued to mix odd-smelling concoctions in test tubes, while barely getting by in school.

Sara Turing, in particular, was concerned about Alan's future. He was at the age where he would graduate from preparatory school and move on to a public school. (In the British school system, a public school is actually a private school with a tuition.) Alan's mother feared that he would become a social outcast at his new school. She explained:

>   Though he had been loved and understood in the narrower homely circle of his preparatory school it was because I foresaw the possible difficulties for the staff and himself at a public school that I was at such pains to find the right one for him, lest if he failed in adaptation to public school life he might become a mere intellectual crank.

Sara Turing eventually settled on the Sherborne School in southwest England; it was this school to which Alan made his celebrated bicycle ride. Although he initially made a splash with that feat, he soon found himself feeling lonely and isolated. Sherborne School stressed discipline and conformity, a culture to which Alan was not well suited. His instructors found him unkempt and withdrawn, not at all the proper English boy. Yet they also found it difficult to criticize his mathematical and scientific abilities, saying only that he should spend more time learning the fundamentals before moving on to advanced concepts.

While Alan's mother fretted over his social life, his father worried about Alan's poor grades. Enrollment at Sherborne

Grasping Einstein's Theories

Around age fifteen Alan Turing began studying the work of Albert Einstein. Specifically, he read *Relativity: The Special and the General Theory*, which had first been published in English in 1920. Such reading was not part of the Sherborne School curriculum; Turing pursued it independently. Not only did he understand the difficult concepts that Einstein discussed in the book, he also grasped what Einstein did not say.

Albert Einstein questioned whether Newton's laws of motion—that an object in motion tends to stay in motion, and an object at rest tends to stay at rest, unless an outside force acts upon it, for example—were true at extremely high speeds or with extremely small objects.

A great deal had been learned about the principles of motion since Isaac Newton put forth his axioms in 1687. While Newton's theories described the motion of typical objects under normal circumstances, Einstein realized that they were not universal. But Einstein never specifically stated his conclusions for a new law of motion in *Relativity: The Special and the General Theory*.

As he read the book Turing had his own ideas about the new laws of motion. In his scribbled notes about Einstein's book Turing wrote, "[Einstein] has now got to find the general law of motion for bodies. It will have, of course, to satisfy the general Principle of Relativity. He does not actually give the law, which I think is a pity, so I will. It is: 'The separation between any two events in the history of a particle shall be a maximum or minimum when measured along its world line.'"

It was part of Turing's nature to question what others took for granted, and he admired Einstein for boldly questioning the Newtonian laws. The fact that a teenager could delve so deeply into theoretical physics was early evidence of Alan Turing's genius.

Albert Einstein
(Library of Congress)

did not come cheaply, and Julius Turing wanted to see some positive results for his money. Both parents remained supportive, but privately they hoped that Alan would become more like his older brother. John was athletic, brought home good marks, and was studying to become an attorney. Sara Turing coached Alan on keeping his clothes neat and tidy, while his father tried to pass along his passion for literature. Neither found very much success.

There was one person who could convince Alan Turing to change his ways, but he was not a parent, sibling, or teacher. He was a fellow student at Sherborne, Christopher Morcom. Although Christopher was a year older and more outgoing than Alan, the two shared a love of mathematics and chemistry. Through their time studying together and discussing mathematical concepts, they became close friends. An accomplished piano player, Christopher attempted to introduce his friend to the world of music, but the nuances of harmony and melody did not appeal to Alan. Christopher had far better luck with astronomy, and soon Alan was immersed in the

Alan (far left) walking with his school friends in 1926. *(Courtesy of King's College Library, Cambridge)*

study of telescopes and star charts.

But Alan's friendship with Christopher Morcom was based on more than just an enjoyment of science. By this time, Alan had reached his early teens and was becoming aware he was different from the other boys at Sherborne School. He had always held different views and interests from those around him, but this was more profound. Alan realized that he did not share his classmates' growing interest in girls. Whereas the young men of Sherborne were attracted to young women, Alan Turing found that he was attracted to other males. Specifically, he was attracted to his good friend Christopher Morcom.

Morcom did not reciprocate Alan's romantic interest, but did not allow it to ruin their friendship. They continued to compare notes on various chemistry experiments, mathematical problems, and astronomical observations.

Morcom began studying for the entrance examinations to college when he was eighteen and, although he was a year younger, Turing decided to do the same. The Sherborne instructors noticed a new seriousness in Turing's work and his grades improved. In the end, though, he did not score well enough on the examinations to advance to college a year early. Morcom earned a scholarship to the University of Cambridge's Trinity College.

Turing was disheartened at being separated from his good friend. But a greater tragedy loomed. Three weeks into his final term at Sherborne, Morcom became seriously ill and went to London for surgery. He continued to deteriorate and all attempts to save his life failed. On February 13, 1930, Morcom died from bovine tuberculosis, which he had contracted as a child after drinking infected milk.

Turing was crushed. While mourning the loss, he wrote to the Morcom family and expressed his condolences, initiating a lifelong friendship with Christopher's mother. He made several visits to the Morcom family home in Worcestershire.

Although Christopher Morcom had been a part of Turing's life for only a few years, he had made a significant impact. Aside from being Turing's first love, Morcom had shown him how to accept responsibility and to apply discipline to his work. Furthermore, his friend's death prompted Turing to think about philosophical concepts, such as destiny and the relationship between the body and the spirit. Turing did not subscribe to any particular religion, but he did allow for the possible existence of a soul. Maybe the body was little more than a "mechanism for the soul? "As regards the question of why we have bodies at all; why we do not or cannot live free as spirits and communicate as such, we probably could do so but there would be nothing whatever to do," he wrote in a letter to Mrs. Morcom. "The body provides something for the spirit to look after and use."

As he began his final year at Sherborne, Turing commanded respect. His intellectual ability was now legendary and as one of the senior students, he was responsible for keeping the younger boys in line. This meant administering corporal punishment and subjecting the newcomers to a variety of hazing rituals. Turing frowned on these practices and avoided them whenever possible. He preferred to spend his time on a newfound hobby—long-distance running. The solitary nature of the sport appealed to him, and lengthy jaunts through the countryside allowed him to work off some of his frustrations.

In December 1930, Turing received a scholarship to King's College, Cambridge. While this was an impressive achievement, King's was not his first choice. He wanted a scholarship to Trinity College, which Christopher Morcom had received.

As a youngster, Alan Turing had been forced to live within the confining rules of a rigid school system. In college, he would find greater freedom to explore his ideas. In this more open academic environment, he would lay a solid foundation for his greatest work.

two

Universal Turing Machine

As in the past, Alan Turing felt like a stranger when he arrived at his new school, but the scholarly atmosphere of King's College offered him hope. The mathematics department was among the best in the nation, and he was able to attend lectures by some of Europe's leading mathematicians. Turing also made some attempts to connect with his new world. He befriended another math scholar, David Champernowne, and he joined the school's boat club. Boating came naturally to Turing, as he had spent much of his life near the coast.

In 1933, Turing joined a political group called the Anti-War Council. As he explained in a letter to his mother, "Its programme is principally to organize strikes amongst munitions and chemical workers when government intends to go to war." Membership in the Anti-War Council was a rare

A view of King's College, Cambridge

departure for Turing. He preferred the certainty of numbers and scientific facts, steadfastly avoiding any opinion-based activity such as politics.

Turing's brief foray into politics was in keeping with the era. The 1930s were a time of social upheaval in Europe. The Great Depression had left millions broke, unemployed, and homeless. World War I was still a fresh and painful memory, but the clouds of war never seemed far off. The anxiety about the future was palatable and even the habitually apolitical Turing decided to take a stand. He was not pleased by what he encountered during a sightseeing tour of Germany in 1934. That nation had fallen under the sway of the Nazi Party and its supreme leader Adolf Hitler.

Outside of his academic work, Turing's undergraduate years at King's College were uneventful. He refused to con-

Adolf Hitler *(Library of Congress)*

fine himself to the abstract side of mathematics and wanted to understand how math applied to the physical world. Mathematicians of the time usually specialized in either theoretical or applied mathematics, but Turing studied both disciplines. This led him to the relatively new field of quantum mechanics, which examines the behavior of atoms and subatomic particles. He was especially interested in how the atoms of the human brain worked together to produce thoughts.

Turing excelled in his work and studies, and before long there was talk of a fellowship position for him at King's College following graduation. His intellectual progress was not matched by greater ease in social situations, however. Although he spent some time in the company of his rowing teammates and fellow math scholars, for the most part he remained isolated. His room was a maelstrom of papers, books, and dirty clothes. Only rarely did he step outside his scholarly persona, as when he purchased a used violin and took a few lessons. In 1934, at the age of twenty-two, he asked his parents for a teddy bear as a Christmas present.

In the spring of 1935, Turing was awarded a fellowship at King's College. The position carried no real duties and came with a small stipend, essentially freeing Turing to pursue his academic interests. He started by submitting a paper to the London Mathematical Society. It was a minor work dealing with periodic functions, but it became Turing's first published paper. He then turned his attention to his favorite subject—how humans think and how a machine might be able to simulate that process.

Alan Turing was not the first person to conceive the idea of a thinking machine. The English mathematician Charles Babbage proposed his "analytical engine" roughly a century earlier. Although never built, Babbage's analytical engine could theoretically perform complex calculations by reading punch cards. Babbage and others had put forth some remarkable ideas about thinking machines, but these did not influence Turing (though he was probably aware of their work). He started by looking at examples of the machines around him.

The typewriter was a common machine in Turing's world, but it performed no calculations. It merely printed a symbol when a typist pressed the corresponding key. By 1935, mechanical calculators existed, but these were simple, gear-operated devices—more like a cash register than the human mind. Turing envisioned a machine that could make decisions based on the specific

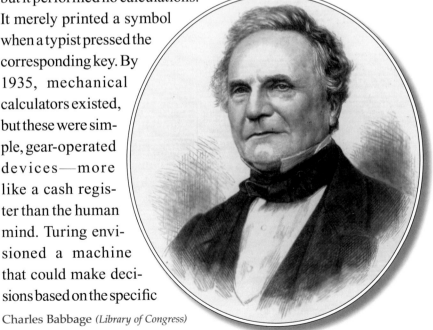

Charles Babbage (*Library of Congress*)

instructions it had been given. But rather than trying to build such a machine, he thought about how it would operate and what instructions he would give it.

Turing's theoretical machine would scan a paper tape as the tape passed through it. In addition to reading what was printed on the paper tape, the machine would be able to write on the tape, erase items from it, and change the direction of the tape whenever instructed to do so. As for the paper tape itself, Turing said that it would be marked off into individual squares, and that each square could either contain a symbol or be left blank. Essentially, the tape would be Turing's means of communicating with his machine. As the machine scanned each square, it would receive information on what to do next. For example, if the machine read a square and found a "1" printed there, it would then refer to its instructions on what to do when encountering a "1."

A machine has no knowledge: before it can execute any task, it must be told precisely what to do. Turing thought of his machine as an unskilled worker who needs exact instructions before performing any job. Also like a human, the machine could be "taught" how to perform a variety of jobs. For example, a person can be given a group of numbers and shown how to add those figures, subtract, multiply, divide, and so forth. Turing referred to the various operations as different "states of mind," and he supposed that his machine could shift its state of mind when told to do so. Accordingly, a typical command for a Turing machine might be, "If your state is 13 and you scan a '1' on the tape, replace the '1' with a '0', move one square to the right, and change your state to 22."

Turing called his machine a "universal machine" because it would be capable of performing any operation for which it received a table of instructions. Turing did not build his machine, but it was a major theoretical step toward the creation of the modern computer. His simple, concise logic helped other thinkers grasp the potential of mechanical computation. Experts in artificial intelligence and computer theory still study Turing's thinking.

Although his universal machine did not exist, Turing could still use it to examine complex mathematical problems. He could predict the machine's behavior based on the rules that governed it. In 1936, he used the rules of the Turing machine to answer a fundamental question about mathematics—the Entscheidungs Problem—German for "decision problem." The Entscheidungs Problem asked whether a method existed for determining whether any given mathematical statement was true or false. In other words, could all problems in mathematics be solved? The question had existed for centuries, but the early 1900s saw a renewed interest in it. The German mathematician David Hilbert firmly believed that a method did, in fact, exist that could solve any problem. In 1930, he even went so far as to state that there was no such thing as an unsolvable mathematical problem.

If Hilbert's assertions were true, Alan Turing reasoned, his universal machine should eventually be able to solve any mathematical problem given to it. Upon reaching the solution, the machine would halt. Although the Turing machine did not exist, logically, if a person looked at the mathematical problem, and then looked at the machine's instruction table, he or she should be able to tell when the machine would arrive at a solution and halt.

Remarkably, Turing discovered that the machine's halting point could not always be found. With some math problems, there was no way to tell whether the machine would find an answer and halt, or simply work away forever without finding a solution. The machine might get caught in a loop or run into some other logic problem that would prevent it from reaching a conclusion. Turing called this the "halting problem," and said it was proof that unsolvable problems do exist. For a twenty-three-year-old graduate student, this was an astounding accomplishment. Turing put his findings into a paper titled "On Computable Numbers, with an Application to the Entscheidungsproblem," which he finished in May 1936.

David Hilbert

Turing decided to go to the United States. New Jersey's Princeton University hosted a multitude of brilliant mathematicians, physicists, and logicians, including the most famous of them all—Albert Einstein. Einstein—like many other German scientists and intellectuals of Jewish descent—had fled Germany after the Nazis came to power. His presence at Princeton signaled the university's growing reputation as the center of the mathematical universe, and Alan Turing wished to be part of that environment.

There was another reason for Turing to go to Princeton University. Shortly after completing his paper on the

Turing (middle) eats cake with a couple of his colleagues during his time at Princeton University. *(Courtesy of King's College Library, Cambridge)*

Entscheidungs Problem, he learned of an American logician named Alonzo Church who taught at Princeton. Coincidentally, Turing and Church had been working on the Entscheidungs Problem at the same time. In fact, Church completed his paper on the subject one month before Turing. Although both men arrived at the same conclusion—that unsolvable problems do exist—they employed different methods to reach that conclusion. While Turing had used his theoretical machine, Church had used a new type of mathematics called lambda calculus. Despite their different approaches, it was clear that Church and Turing had much in common and might collaborate to develop their theory even further.

In September 1936, Turing boarded an ocean liner bound for the United States. Almost immediately after his arrival, Turing noticed some cultural differences between the United States and his native Britain. In contrast to the formality and natural reserve of the English, Turing found Americans relaxed and gregarious, which he appreciated. "The graduate students," he reported to his mother, "include a very large number who are working in mathematics and none of them mind talking shop. It is very different from Cambridge in that way." Yet Turing had little time for small talk, preferring that the loquacious Americans stick to discussing their scholarly pursuits. He grumbled about a dinner party he attended at Alonzo Church's house. The guest list included many important names from the university, so Turing assumed that the dinner conversation would revolve around lofty ideas. Instead, he listened gloomily as people talked about their hometowns and various trips they had taken. "Description of travel and places bores me intensely," Turing told his mother.

Overall, Turing enjoyed his time at Princeton. He worked alone and with Church, and attended the lectures of the pioneering mathematicians who had drawn him there. In the spring of 1937, he bought a used car and had a friend teach him to drive. Turing's clumsiness made this a bit of a challenge, but eventually he felt confident enough for a trip to Rhode Island, where he visited some distant relatives from his mother's side of the family.

As Turing entered his second year at Princeton, international tensions were on the rise. Nazi Germany was growing ever more bellicose, and Turing—like others—believed that another war between Europe's major powers was likely. He knew that in the event of such a conflict, the British government would have a pressing need for people expert in the field of cryptography.

Cryptography is the study and practice of secret communication through the use of codes and ciphers. While the terms are often used interchangeably, codes and ciphers are technically not the same. In a code, each word in a text to be encrypted is replaced by a symbol, number, or other word that has arbitrarily been assigned that word's meaning. Typically, the code words and their plain-language equivalents are found in a codebook that may be thought of as a dictionary available only to the sender and recipient of the encoded message. Just as dictionary entries and their definitions do not change, code words do not vary as long as a specific code is in use. In a cipher, by contrast, a variable key determines how the plain-language text will be encrypted—typically, each letter of each word is rearranged or replaced with another letter, number, or set of numbers. For a cipher system to work, both the sender and the recipient of a message must know the key.

The practice of sending encrypted messages is nearly as ancient as warfare itself. A successfully encrypted message must yield no valuable information to an enemy who intercepts it. At the same time, the intended recipient must know how to read the message in order for it to be useful. The Roman leader Julius Caesar communicated with his generals using a "shift" cipher. This technique merely substituted each letter in the message with another letter farther down in the alphabet. The key to Caesar's cipher, which the sender and receiver agreed on in advance, was the number of positions to shift in the alphabet while encoding and decoding. So, for example, if the key was three and Caesar sent a message that read, "dwwdfn qrz," his generals would decipher it as "attack now."

By 1937, when Alan Turing began to take a keen interest in cryptography, methods of encryption were significantly more sophisticated. A cipher as simple as Caesar's would be broken in moments by anyone competent in cryptanalysis, or the solving of codes and ciphers. Modern ciphers were polyalphabetic, meaning that multiple keys were employed within the same message, sometimes even changing with each letter. While exceedingly complex, even these methods were not impervious to decryption because of the underlying patterns in language.

As was his nature, Turing approached the problem from a different angle. He decided to devise a cipher system using some elementary, but little-known, applications of mathematics. Turing began by creating a key for transforming the letters of a message into numbers. He then expressed those numbers in binary form. (The expression of numbers as a series of two symbols, typically "1" and "0," is fundamental to all modern computers, but in 1937 it was still considered a novelty.) Binary numbers enabled Turing to introduce an electrical machine into his encryption system. The binary "1" and "0" could easily be represented to a machine in many ways, such as a switch being in the "on" or "off" position, or a circuit being "open" or "closed." Turing designed a machine he called the "electric multiplier" that would multiply the numbers of a message by a second key, which was a large number of his choosing. The product of this mathematical operation would then be transmitted as the encoded message. Turing estimated that it would take an enemy who intercepted the message roughly one hundred years to decipher it—and that was assuming the enemy possessed his original key, which changed the letters into numbers.

Like the Turing machine, his mathematical cipher system was a thought exercise—a tool to aid in understanding.

Regardless, Turing was curious enough about his electric multiplier to sneak into Princeton's machine shop and construct the first few stages of it. He was pleasantly surprised to discover that it worked.

Princeton awarded Turing his doctoral degree in June 1938 and offered him a position at the university, but he declined. The political situation in Europe was deteriorating, and he felt the need to return to his native land. He hoped that his cipher system would be able to be put to good use.

Computers and the Algorithm

An algorithm is a clearly defined procedure for arriving at a desired result, akin to a recipe. In mathematics, algorithms are widely used to solve routine problems. Anyone who has performed long division, for example, has used a basic algorithm. The idea dates back to the ninth century in the Middle East, where shepherds employed simple rules of arithmetic to keep track of their flocks. However, the algorithm concept was not formally defined until the first half of the twentieth century, and Alan Turing played a pivotal role in that process.

The Turing machine clarified the requirements for mechanical computation. Turing's theoretical machine would require precise instructions. The instructions needed to be placed in the correct order, and they needed to account for all of the different possibilities the machine might encounter during the operation. Finally, the end of the process would need to be clearly stated. Within this framework, the algorithm came to be thought of as any complete computational process that can be performed mechanically, whether by human or machine.

Enhancements to the algorithm definition have been developed since Turing's time, and there are now many different classifications. Today's complex algorithms routinely contain other algorithms, but the basic premise remains the same. Computer programmers make extensive use of algorithms in their work. In fact, an entire computer program, such as a video game, may be considered an algorithm because the program tells the computer precisely how to run the game from beginning to end.

Slightly more than a year after Turing graduated, on September 1, 1939, German forces invaded Poland, triggering the largest military conflict in human history. Previously, Alan Turing's imaginative and abstract ideas had little impact on the everyday world. During World War II, his innovative work would help decide the fate of entire continents.

three
Unraveling
the Enigma

When Alan Turing returned to Great Britain in the summer of 1938 he went to work for the Government Code and Cypher School. ("Cypher" is the British spelling of "cipher.") The agency was small and poorly funded, but new cryptanalysts were needed to study the mounting volume of German military signals. Turing's reputation had preceded him across the Atlantic, and he was promptly recruited into the project.

Following the official declaration of war in September 1939, the Government Code and Cypher School moved to a secret location forty-five miles from London. Known as Bletchley Park, the facility was little more than a country estate with a Victorian mansion and several outbuildings. However, the mysterious Bletchley Park would become a codebreaking nerve center during the war, as well as Turing's home for the next several years.

The mansion at Bletchley Park

The German military used a variety of ciphers to encode its communications, but the most difficult to crack was called the Enigma. German cryptographers were convinced their code could not be broken and for a while the frustrated cryptanalysts at Bletchley were starting to agree. An electric machine containing a series of mechanical rotors and resembling a typewriter produced the Enigma cipher and even the experienced codebreakers began to think the Enigma device worked in a system that would always seem random to anyone without the key.

In order for the encryption system to work, both sender and recipient first needed an Enigma machine, and they had to ensure that the rotor settings of both machines matched exactly. If, for example, the sender pressed the "G" button on his keyboard, the machine might display a "Z." Provided that the recipient used the same rotor settings, he could then press the "Z" button on his keyboard and see a "G" light up on his machine's display.

The Enigma machine itself was not new. It had been invented in 1923 and was available for purchase commercially around the world. Banks, post offices, and other businesses requiring secure communications used it. Of course, simply owning an Enigma machine was not enough to decipher messages; one also had to know the rotor settings of the sender's machine—the key to the system. Each Enigma machine contained three rotors, and each rotor had twenty-six different settings. This meant that the trio of rotors could be placed in any one of 17,576 different configurations (26 x 26 x 26 = 17,576). Only an Enigma machine placed in the exact configuration used by the sender could properly decode

A German Enigma machine

a message. A machine in any other configuration would produce unintelligible nonsense.

The Germans made their Enigma machines even more complex. Aside from dutifully changing the rotor settings each day, they introduced two additional rotors. The Enigma machine could accept only three rotors at a time, but the British cryptanalysts had no way of knowing which three of the five rotors the German operators were using at any given time. Additionally, the Germans added a new piece of hardware to their machines called a plugboard. The plugboard, which attached to the front of the machine, was electrically wired to the rotors and contained twenty-six jacks into which cables could be plugged. By plugging the cables into different jacks, the Germans added yet another element of randomness to their system. Instead of 17,576 different configurations, the German Enigma machine was capable of well over a trillion.

At Bletchley Park, Alan Turing went to work in Hut 8, a small outbuilding where haggard cryptanalysts desperately tried to decipher messages intercepted from the German navy. German submarines, or U-boats, were sinking British cargo ships at an alarming rate, threatening to starve the island nation into submission. Because deciphered messages would reveal U-boat locations, Bletchley Park assigned top priority to cracking the German navy's Enigma—but the task seemed impossible.

Before the outbreak of the war, several cryptanalysts in Poland had made some fundamental discoveries about Enigma. The Poles had shared these findings with their British counterparts before the invasion of Poland in September 1939.

German Luftwaffe troops using an Enigma machine to send a coded message. *(Courtesy of Helge Fykse/U.S. Air Force)*

The Polish cryptanalysts used a modern branch of mathematics known as group theory, as well as information about Enigma obtained from spies, along with a little guesswork, to deduce how the German-modified Enigma machine operated. They learned that Enigma would never encode a letter as itself, and that German operators routinely included clues about the rotor setting they were using at the start of each message to ensure that the message's intended recipient had the correct rotor setting.

This inside knowledge of how the German's operated the Enigma machine eliminated some of its random elements, but it was not enough to crack the cipher. To do this, they would have to try every possible remaining rotor setting manually until they stumbled across the one that deciphered a particular message. Ingeniously, the Poles built electrical machines to simulate each rotor setting. The machines were dubbed bombes, from the French word for bomb. According to some accounts, the name originated because they sounded like ticking time bombs as they laboriously clicked through each possible setting; other accounts say the nickname derived from the Polish cryptanalysts' love of a frozen dessert known as a bombe. In any case, the strides made by the Polish cryptanalysts provided a solid foundation upon which Alan Turing and his associates at Bletchley Park could use to decipher Enigma.

The Bombes of Bletchley

Decrypting Enigma messages was a constant struggle for the mathematicians of Bletchley Park. The first of the British bombes went into operation in the spring of 1940. Progress was slow. During that first year, Bletchley Park decrypted only 273 German Enigma messages. In 1941, that number increased to 1,344, and in 1942 a total of 4,655 messages were decrypted.

As U-boat losses mounted while the number of British cargo ships sent to the bottom declined, German naval commanders started to suspect their Enigma system might have been compromised. Accordingly, they ordered a series of modifications to thwart codebreaking. This meant the Bletchley cryptanalysts were constantly trying to adjust their bombes to compensate for each new German tactic. As always, they resorted to trial-and-error methods, which sometimes took months.

Alan Turing realized that mathematics could speed the process. Previously, the cryptanalysts would try a new crib, rotor setting, or other potential solution merely because it seemed likely to work. Turing wanted to quantify the probability of success of each potential solution so the likeliest solutions could be tried first. He likened the concept to that of the odds in gambling. He wanted to know the odds in the Enigma game so he could bet on the best potential solutions. Instead of winning money, Bletchley Park would win valuable time. In the deadly U-boat war, an hour saved could mean the difference between destruction or escape for a British convoy.

Turing began to assign numerical values to the various bits of evidence the cryptanalysts collected. All the bits of evidence that supported a particular solution could then be added up. Any potential solution possessing a high enough probability figure was deemed worth trying. Possible solutions with a low score were set aside for later. The procedure worked, and the cryptanalysts started finding the correct answers sooner. Turing had essentially replaced human intuition with a mathematical process. Today, the concept is known as sequential analysis.

A woman working at a bombe machine. *(Courtesy of U.S. Air Force)*

Turing loved the environment at Bletchley. He was surrounded by like-minded individuals and it was obvious to everyone that their work was critically important. What they did at Bletchley Park could win the war. This unrelenting urgency of the situation thrilled Turing. He was always happiest when solving a problem with real-world applications. Not only was the Enigma problem real, it demanded the creative use of logic and mathematics—an arena in which Turing excelled. Ironically, although he despised war, it provided him with the perfect job.

However, Turing was not always optimistic about Great Britain's chances for survival. Throughout the spring of 1940, the German war machine raced across continental Europe, halting only at the English Channel. Invasion seemed imminent; German bombers appeared over London and other British population centers. Fearing the collapse of the British banking system, Turing decided it might be wise to stash his meager savings elsewhere. He purchased two bars of silver and buried them at a secret spot in the woods. In typical Turing fashion, he made detailed notes about the location and encrypted them. Sadly for him, he failed to consider that the forest landscape might change dramatically over time. Several postwar expeditions into the woods failed to yield his silver bars.

Meanwhile, at Bletchley Park, the cryptanalysts were building a fleet of sixty bombes to decipher the German Enigma traffic. It was a huge undertaking, and would not be enough. Even with five-dozen machines continuously clicking away, it still might take several days to find the correct rotor setting for a particular message. By then, the information contained in the message was probably useless because U-boats were constantly on the move. The cryptanalysts had to find a way to decipher messages in hours, not days.

Alan Turing suspected that the way to accomplish this was by exploiting Germany's blind faith in Enigma. Normally, a good cipher clerk avoids using the same words and phrases repeatedly when writing messages. The overuse of identical wording would leave the messages vulnerable to a decryption method known as "probable-word attack." A cryptanalyst using probable-word attack knows that certain words and phrases appear frequently in most communications. Examples of commonly used words would be "the," "that," and "here," while "Sincerely yours" is a frequently used phrase. If the cryptanalyst can correctly identify a frequently used word or phrase in an encoded message, he or she has uncovered part of the key for decoding the entire message.

An Enigma message that has been decrypted by codebreakers at Bletchley Park. *(Courtesy of Dr. David Hamer/U.S. Air Force)*

The Germans were so confident in Enigma that they often ignored the basic rules of cryptography. Cipher clerks routinely used the same words repeatedly. Some military units methodically included the Nazi salute "Heil Hitler!" in every message and routinely repeated long phrases, such as "The weather forecast for today . . . " For a clever cryptanalyst such as Alan Turing, this was an exploitable mistake.

Turing designed the British bombes to look for probable words and phrases. It was not easy because a human would first need to identify a possible word match in the enciphered message. The British referred to matched words as "cribs" because they were like crib sheets—cheats—for deciphering the message. A correctly guessed crib would enable the bombes to eliminate billions of possible Enigma configurations. They could then try out the remaining configurations until the right one revealed itself.

The bombes were intricate machines. Each was roughly the height and weight of a large refrigerator, but more than twice as wide, and bristled with plugs and cables. Each contained slots for no less than 108 Enigma-like rotors and required a small army of clerical workers to look after them. Unfortunately, in wartime England, few skilled workers were still available. Most were serving in the military or working in essential industries. The Bletchley Park cryptanalysts pleaded with the government for more clerks, but none arrived. Finally, Turing and his colleagues grew so desperate that they took the bold step of sending a letter directly to Prime Minister Winston Churchill. They wrote:

> Dear Prime Minister,
> Some weeks ago you paid us the honour of a visit, and we

believe that you regard our work as important. You will have seen that . . . we have been well supplied with the 'bombes' for the breaking of the German Enigma codes. We think, however, that you ought to know that this work is being held up, and in some cases is not being done at all, principally because we cannot get sufficient staff to deal with it. Our reason for writing to you direct is that for months we have done everything that we possibly can through the normal channels, and that we despair of any early improvement without your intervention.

Winston Churchill knew Bletchley Park was crucial to the British war effort and, after receiving the letter, ordered that the cryptanalysts should have every resource they needed, including the necessary clerical workers. The job fell to the volunteers of the Women's Royal Naval Service. These dedicated women learned to load rotors into slots, manage a jumble of cables, and do whatever else was necessary to keep the odd, clicking machines running.

Winston Churchill (*Library of Congress*)

As the project's leader, Alan Turing was responsible for overseeing the women's work. Not surprisingly, he was uncomfortable in this role. He had lived most of his twenty-eight years at various boys' schools and male-dominated colleges, and had little experience interacting with women. Now he was in charge of an entire roomful of them. He kept a low profile, emerging

Codebreakers at work in a Bletchley Park hut *(Courtesy of Bletchley Park Trust/SSPL/The Image Works)*

from his office only when necessary. The shy, retiring young man reminded Bletchley Park's workers of a university professor, and they affectionately referred to him as "Prof," a nickname that embarrassed him immensely.

There was one woman who cut through Turing's shyness. Joan Clarke was not part of the clerical staff. She was a mathematician who worked alongside Turing in Hut 8. The two developed a comfortable friendship, playing chess in their free time and taking bicycle rides through the country. In 1941, Turing surprised Clarke with a proposal of marriage. He warned her about what he termed his homosexual tendencies, but she was undaunted and accepted. They happily talked about the future, when the war was finally over. Turing even revealed that he would someday like to have children.

Any plans for a family would have to wait. Britain was engaged in a fierce struggle for survival, and there was much codebreaking to be done. In March 1941, Hitler's troops spread throughout North Africa. Three months later, Germany invaded the Soviet Union, unexpectedly drawing that mammoth nation into the war. Meanwhile, Germany's powerful Pacific ally, Japan, wreaked havoc throughout Asia and on December 7, 1941, the Japanese navy attacked the American naval base at Pearl Harbor in Hawaii. The surprise assault propelled the United States into the war.

German U-boats began patrolling the waters off the eastern United States, sinking American cargo ships. During the first four months of 1942, more than 150 ships were sunk. U.S. officials appealed to their British allies for help in combating the U-boats. The British agreed to share what they had learned about the German Enigma and offered the United States help on building its own bombes. To accomplish this, Bletchley Park decided to send its premier cryptanalyst to Washington, D.C. Alan Turing packed his bags for another voyage to the United States.

four

Beyond Bletchley Park

Those who knew Alan Turing wondered how he would be received in the United States. He did not always make a good first impression, and his ragged fingernails, gray teeth, and nervous laugh did not immediately inspire confidence. Such confidence came later, when his razor-sharp intellect became apparent.

The administrators of Bletchley Park had generally overlooked his quirks. They allowed him to work at odd hours, especially late at night, and did not make an issue of his often-bizarre form of dress—co-workers reported seeing Turing using a length of twine as a belt or wearing a pajama top beneath his sport jacket.

Turing could create real trouble for those in charge. One incident demonstrated this clearly, and also typified his general outlook on life. The codebreakers of Bletchley Park were government-employed civilians, but were also encouraged to become part-time soldiers. Turing was interested in learning how to shoot a rifle and agreed to join Britain's Home Guard, which was akin to the National Guard in the United States. A question on the application asked, "Do you understand that by enrolling in the Home Guard you place yourself liable to military law?" Whereas most new recruits automatically checked "Yes" to this question, Turing checked "No." The officer collecting the applications never noticed Turing's negative response, and military training for the codebreakers commenced.

Turing learned how to use a rifle and eventually became quite a sharpshooter. Upon accomplishing his goal, he became bored with the mundane routine of military inspections and parades and stopped attending. He was soon hauled before his commanding officer to explain his absences. He respectfully told the colonel that he had only joined the Home Guard to learn marksmanship and now saw no reason to continue. The increasingly agitated colonel informed Turing he had no choice in the matter. Military law required recruits to attend all drills. Turing politely responded that he was not subject to military law, as noted on his application. The now red-faced colonel reviewed the form and abruptly sent Turing away. His brief military career was over.

As long as Turing continued to produce results his superiors would tolerate his antics and eccentricities, though. His American handlers would find it sensible to adopt the same attitude.

Turing arrived in New York Harbor on November 13, 1942, and traveled to Washington, D.C., to meet with the U.S. Navy's top cryptanalysts. The Americans were planning a bombe program even larger than that of Bletchley Park.

More than one hundred larger, heavier American bombes would supplement the British machines already in operation. Within six weeks, Turing had his American counterparts up to speed. He then returned to New York to commence work on a new project.

His latest interest took him from trying to break encryption systems to inventing new ones. Specifically, he sought to create a method by which the human voice could be reliably encrypted for transmission. If possible, speech encryption would have countless military applications. It would also help the U.S. and British governments communicate more effectively across the Atlantic Ocean. Engineers at Bell Laboratories in New York City were working on the problem, and Turing hoped to learn from them.

During his time at the bustling Bell Laboratories, Turing learned a great deal about this new field. He also forged some valuable friendships. However, some employees misinterpreted

In 1942, Turing spent time at Bell Laboratories learning about voice encryption technology. *(Courtesy of AP Images/Angel Franco)*

his unusual nature as arrogance. When a friend took him aside and asked why he did not acknowledge acquaintances in the hallway, Turing was surprised. He said he had not intended to be impolite. To him, constantly greeting people seemed both unnecessary and redundant. He nevertheless made a conscious effort to say hello from that point forward.

Turing departed New York in March 1943 aboard a troop-transport ship bound for England that was packed with 4,000 U.S. soldiers. The rugged American infantrymen would play a role in the D-Day invasion of Nazi-occupied France the following year. The quiet, pale Englishman in their midst had already made enormous contributions to the war effort. He had, in fact, helped make the Atlantic crossing safer for United States soldiers and sailors.

Nevertheless, U-boat "wolf packs" still infested the Atlantic in 1943, making the sea journey between the United States and England precarious. Turing's voyage proceeded without incident, however.

Back at Bletchley, Turing slowly withdrew from the daily grind of deciphering messages. The other cryptanalysts still consulted him whenever a thorny problem arose, but primarily he worked alone, focusing on other challenges. His official responsibilities now lay in developing a voice encryption system. To that end, he taught himself the basics of electronics. Electronic devices, as the name implies, use the flow of electrons to generate, transmit, receive, and store information. Interestingly, a distant relative of Alan Turing's mother coined the term electron. In 1894, physicist George Johnstone Stoney first used the word to describe subatomic particles that carry an electrical charge. In the 1940s, electronics was still a very new branch of physics and engineering. Though he was not an engineer, Turing was intrigued by the seemingly endless possibilities of electronics—and not just for voice encryption. Specifically, he envisioned an electronic brain. As a result, Turing immersed himself in circuits and vacuum tubes.

Turing was now alone not only in his work, but in his personal life as well. His engagement to Joan Clarke had ended. He loved Joan, and he told her so, but as time passed it became painfully clear that any attempt at marriage would fail. Turing could not deny his homosexuality any longer. A union with Joan, or with any woman, could not make him happy. He told Joan that he feared his family would not accept her, but she understood the real reason for their breakup. They remained on cordial terms, but the closeness of their original friendship was gone.

Turing's research continued to expand beyond the daily activities at Bletchley Park. The codebreakers were designing a new machine called Colossus, which would far surpass the capabilities of the original bombes. Turing knew of the project but had no desire to participate in it. Colossus would require him to be part of a team, while his voice encryption project could be pursued alone. When given a choice, Turing always preferred to work by himself. In the fall of 1943, he moved from Bletchley to a different top secret facility ten miles to the north.

Hanslope Park was another old country estate that the government had converted into a wartime intelligence center. Unlike Bletchley, it had a large population of army officers. Not surprisingly, Turing's arrival at the military-minded Hanslope Park caused a stir. His ragged, wrinkled clothes raised the eyebrows of the sharply dressed officers, as did his

The Colossus machine (seen here) was designed by codebreakers to replace the bombe. (*Courtesy of AP Images*)

habit of making a high-pitched clucking sound as he thought through difficult problems. A staff car was available to him, but he preferred the use of his bicycle, even in the rain. During hay fever season, he would often pedal about with a handkerchief tied to his face. As elsewhere, any misgivings about Turing's capabilities, and even his sanity, soon melted away. During his first few days, Turing observed some of the projects under way at Hanslope and proposed ideas to speed their progress. Afterward, his unorthodox appearance and personality were accepted, or at least ignored.

Turing settled down to continue the work on his own project, which now had the code name Delilah. The name—which since biblical times has held connotations of cunning and deception—was suggested by Robin Gandy, a Hanslope Park co-worker whom Turing had known since their days together at King's College. Gandy would become one of the few people to maintain a lifelong friendship with Turing, along with Donald Bayley, an electrical engineer at Hanslope. The challenges of speech encipherment fascinated Bayley, and he pleaded with Turing to allow him to work on the Delilah project. Although Turing had accumulated considerable knowledge of electronics, he was not an engineer, and he accepted Bayley's offer of help.

Together, the mathematician and the engineer attacked the problem of encrypting actual speech, which meant masking the sound of a human voice—with its constantly changing pitch and tone—from everyone but the intended listener. It was far different from anything Turing had previously attempted, and progress was slow. Hanslope colleagues joked about the electronic "bird's nest" of wires and components around which Turing and Bayley seemed forever huddled.

The closeness with which the two men collaborated enabled them to develop a solid friendship. By all accounts, Donald Bayley looked up to the "Prof," as Turing's colleagues continued to call him. Their friendship was damaged, however, when one day Turing offhandedly mentioned his homosexuality. Bayley was the product of a conservative upbringing, and he had not held the slightest suspicion that his working partner was gay. The revelation was a shock, but even more startling to Bayley was Turing's nonchalance toward the matter. For his part, Turing felt hurt by his friend's revulsion at a fundamental part of his being. The two men quarreled for some time before finally agreeing to disagree. Turing concluded that Donald Bayley suffered from the same shortsightedness that afflicted much of the world. Bayley, meanwhile, came to look on Turing's homosexuality as just another of his many quirks.

In the end, Turing and Bayley managed to make their complex machine work. In March 1944, they transmitted a recording of a recent radio speech by Winston Churchill. To anyone listening the transmission sounded like static, but transformed the white noise back into the voice of the prime minister. Despite this remarkable accomplishment, Delilah had drawbacks. It did not work well with long-distance radio transmissions. The biggest problem, however, was timing. Delilah appeared too late in the war to be of significant value.

By the spring of 1944, the tide had turned in favor of the Allies. The menacing threat of a German invasion of England had passed. Hitler's once mighty U-boats were no longer the hunters of the Atlantic, but had turned into the hunted. Soviet forces pressed on Germany from the east and in the west, American, British, and Canadian troops were assembling for the largest seaborne invasion in history to take place at Normandy, in France. Within a year, the crushing assault from two fronts would force Germany to capitulate. Delilah was no longer needed, and the laborious creation of Turing and Bayley faded into oblivion.

Turing was disappointed that an entire year of grueling work could not be used, but the effort had not been entirely in vain. He had furthered his understanding of electronics and developed new concepts on which to build. Now that war was ending he was free to explore his own interests. Chief among these was his long-standing desire to construct a machine capable of simulating human thought. Even before the guns of Europe had gone silent, Turing was once again shifting his attention. He was now obsessed with the notion of building a brain.

The Delilah Project

The purpose of the top secret Delilah machine was to create a secure mode of voice communication. The concept was not new—engineers at Bell Laboratories first began working on speech encryption in 1928. In 1935, they patented a device called the Vocoder, short for voice encoder. The Vocoder worked, but it gave the speaker's voice a very mechanical sound that was difficult to understand. Turing hoped to produce a system with natural-sounding speech.

Delilah operated on two basic premises, the first of which was called sampling. Rather than transmitting the continuous sound wave of a person's voice, it sampled the voice many times per second and transmitted only those samples. The recipient's Delilah machine would analyze the samples it received, and then fill in the missing data. It was like connecting a series of dots on a sheet of paper, with the samples serving as the dots.

The second premise Turing used was modular arithmetic, in which numbers "wrap around" a specific value. The hands of a clock provide a simple demonstration of modular arithmetic. For example, if four hours are added to ten o'clock, the result is two, not fourteen, because the clock's numbers start over after reaching twelve. Turing used modular arithmetic for encryption. Without knowing the key number (such as twelve, in the case of the clock), an enemy could not decipher a Delilah transmission.

To Turing's chagrin, Delilah was an imperfect system. The slightest time delay between sender and recipient rendered a transmission indecipherable. As a result, Delilah was useless for long-range, shortwave communications. Despite this critical flaw, Delilah was a typical Alan Turing creation. It highlighted his ability to attack a complex problem in the simplest manner. A similar voice encryption system developed in the United States required both sender and recipient to possess an entire roomful of delicate electronics, while Delilah was roughly the size of a large suitcase.

five
Building a Brain

The war in Europe officially ended on May 8, 1945. The colossal struggle that had dominated the past six years of Alan Turing's life, and had threatened the existence of his nation, was finally over. Vicious fighting still raged on in the Pacific, where American forces were steadily reducing Japan's once-extensive empire, but that conflict had little impact on Turing.

In June 1945, in recognition of his contribution to the war effort, Turing was honored with the Order of the British Empire. He was not at liberty to discuss how he had earned the prestigious medal. In fact, the achievements of the Bletchley Park codebreakers would remain top secret for decades. Characteristically, Turing was indifferent to the honor. He placed little value on public recognition and refused to display the medal.

Turing's obligation to the military was finished, but his affiliation with the British government continued. He briefly considered returning to the familiar environment of King's College but decided instead to go somewhere new. His choice was the National Physics Laboratory, or NPL, located in the London suburbs. Although the NPL had a long history as the government's premier research facility, its mathematics division was begun in 1944. The new section's primary goal was to keep pace with the United States in the burgeoning field of electronic computing. Turing had conceived the idea of a universal machine a full decade earlier and was a natural for the job. The NPL researchers rejoiced when he accepted the invitation to join their group.

When Turing talked about "building a brain," he meant to create a reproduction of the human brain. The human brain is a three-pound mass of soft tissue responsible for a multitude of life functions. It controls the body's movement and sleep patterns, and is responsible for sensations such as

A building at the National Physics Laboratory in London, where Turing went to work after WWII.

hunger and thirst. None of these interested Turing. Nor did he care about how or why the brain generates emotions. His focus was entirely on logic. Simply put, Turing wanted to know how the brain makes decisions and arrives at logical conclusions. He wanted to build a machine that could make choices in the same manner that people make choices. He called it "machine intelligence," but the more common term today is artificial intelligence.

In the mid-1940s, the idea of machine intelligence was unfathomable to most people. They knew machines simply as tools that helped humans accomplish tasks. Cars and

Turing's interest in the processes of the human brain led him to believe he could build a machine that could reason and think. *(Courtesy of Carol and Mike Werner/Alamy)*

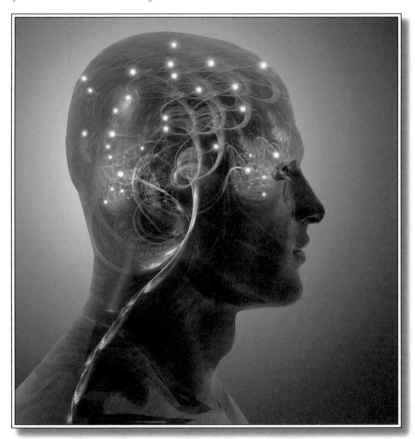

airplanes provided transportation, washing machines cleaned clothes, and lawnmowers cut grass. None of these machines ever made a decision, and they certainly did not possess intelligence. Moreover, the public was completely unaware of the intricate machines that had been invented during the war. The Bletchley bombes, Colossus, and Delilah were still closely guarded government secrets. Therefore, the news that NPL scientists were trying to develop intelligent machines met with considerable skepticism.

To Alan Turing, the notion seemed perfectly rational. "A great positive reason for believing in the possibility of making thinking machinery," he wrote in one paper, "is the fact that it is possible to make machinery to imitate any small part of a man. That the microphone does this for the ear, and the television for the eye, are commonplaces."

The human brain is part of the central nervous system. It contains hundreds of billions of neurons, or nerve cells. The neurons are arranged in circuits and communicate with each other via electrical and chemical impulses. Turing noted that electronic devices also use electrical circuits. However, while a brain's size is limited by the size of the human skull, a machine has no such limitations. An electronic machine, therefore, might be able not only to simulate certain brain functions, but also to perform them faster.

For much of his life, Turing had dwelled on the human capacity for decision making. It was not an easy process to understand. Every day, each person makes countless decisions about what to do, how to dress, what to eat for dinner, and so on. Some choices are elementary, such as the decision to wear a coat on a cold winter day. Other choices appear to be more random, such as which color shirt to buy, and like-minded individuals often make different choices. If three friends go shopping, all three might come home with a different-colored shirt as each individual considers the options available and arrives at a unique conclusion.

In order to simplify the issue, Turing focused his attention on games. Certain games, like tic-tac-toe, have simple, straightforward rules that present players with well-defined choices. Assuming that the player's goal is to win, there are only a few moves to choose from at any given turn in the game. It should therefore be possible, Turing reasoned, to create an automated playing method that a machine could follow. By concentrating on simple games, Turing shrank the universe of human decision making down to a tiny playing board. Instead of tic-tac-toe, he chose to begin his analysis with one of his favorite pastimes—the strategy-rich game of chess.

Turing decided to use the game of chess as a way to test the decision-making skills of his thinking machine.

Historians have traced the origins of chess to sixth-century India, to a military-style board game called *chaturanga*. That game had just four types of pieces, each representing a component of the ancient Indian army: elephants, chariots, cavalry, and infantry. The rules of chess, as they are known today, did not develop until the fifteenth century in Europe. Essentially a game of conquest through battlefield tactics,

Turing and Game Theory

One of the uses of game theory is to help develop winning strategies at games such as chess. However, game theory can be applied to more than just games. Economists, military planners, and politicians, among others, make use of game theory.

The Hungarian American mathematician John von Neumann is widely recognized as the father of game theory. Alan Turing was a student of von Neumann while at Princeton University, and afterward game theory remained one of Turing's favorite topics.

Von Neumann described chess as a game of perfect information because all of the pieces, along with their potential movements, are visible to both players on the chessboard. Poker, on the other hand, is a game of imperfect information because an opponent's hand and the cards to be dealt are hidden from view. As a result, poker players must often rely on bluffing and intuition.

In building his "thinking machine" Turing knew it would be difficult for it to emulate such distinctly human characteristics and stayed with the perfect information of chess. His program, which mapped out all potential moves and assigned them numerical values, enabled a machine to simulate the actions of a human chess player, but Turing knew he had not developed a perfect winning strategy. For example, a skilled player might intentionally sacrifice an important piece in order to draw the machine into a trap. To avoid this, Turing used a game theory concept known as minimax. The goal of the minimax method is to minimize an opponent's maximum gain. In other words, it means leaving an opponent with the worst choices possible, like playing for a tie in tic-tac-toe. Accordingly, Turing's chess-playing machine would not necessarily choose the move that offered it the greatest advantage, but instead choose the move that would leave its opponent with the least advantage.

Turing was never completely satisfied with his chess program. He attributed its shortcomings to his less-than-stellar abilities as a chess player. A few years later, while still waiting for an adequate computer to be built, Turing tried out his chess program on a human player. Turing pretended to be the computer, strictly following the instructions of his program as he moved, while colleague Alick Glennie served as the opposition. The game took hours, as Turing dutifully calculated the computer's moves with paper and pen. Glennie eventually won. However, Turing subsequently repeated the exercise with a lesser opponent, and this time the computer won.

chess was popular with kings and generals alike. It also held appeal (and still does today) for anyone interested in logic and strategic thought. It is little wonder that Alan Turing had been drawn to chess ever since his childhood.

As he had done when imagining the universal Turing machine in 1935, Turing thought of his chess-playing machine as an unskilled human worker. A person who never played chess before, and did not understand its rules, would require precise instructions before moving. So too would Turing's imaginary machine. If he provided it with detailed commands on how to react to an opponent's move, the machine would not need to understand the strategy of the game. It would simply have to execute blindly his instructions for a countermove. However, a chessboard contains sixty-four squares onto which thirty-two pieces are arranged. As the games progresses, pieces travel around the board and are removed from play when captured. The varying number of pieces, and their ever-changing configuration on the chessboard, presented Turing with a problem. The sheer number of potential moves and countermoves would render his instructions staggeringly lengthy.

Turing decided to develop a system to provide his machine with the commands it needed. He first employed a simple analytical tool known as a decision tree. Decision trees help clarify situations that offer many options. The trunk of the tree represents the decision to be made, while a separate branch represents available options. The potential consequences of each option are secondary branches. In Turing's case, the trunk was the alignment of the chess pieces on the board, and the branches were all the legal moves possible.

Next, Turing assigned numerical values to the possible outcomes that a move might yield. For example, capturing an opponent's pawn might be worth twenty points, while capturing a knight might have a value of forty-five points. Placing the opposing king in checkmate would have the highest value of all, since it would win the game. Turing had used the numerical value method before, such as when he streamlined the codebreaking process at Bletchley Park. In that situation, the method had helped the cryptanalysts decide which potential solution to try first when decoding a message. In Turing's chess program, it would enable the machine to choose the best move available.

His elegant procedure formalized the basic mental process that chess players go through when choosing their next move. However, Turing's theoretical chess-playing machine had an advantage—it was capable of looking ahead many moves. An average player might be able to anticipate an opponent's countermove, and then consider the next set of available moves. Beyond that, there are simply too many variables to consider, and the average person quickly becomes overwhelmed. Further, the entire process becomes unhinged when an opponent makes an unexpected move.

A computer, however, is undaunted by a large number of variables. It can follow each branch of the decision tree forward as it grows and splits into many other branches. An opponent's unexpected move cannot surprise a machine, because a machine has no expectations. It has already mapped out every possibility, examined each response, and followed each potential chain of events to its logical conclusion. For Turing, the chess exercise demonstrated the sheer power of electronic computing. A computer might not possess the insight or creativity of a human mind, but it could perform immense calculations with speed and accuracy.

The electronic brain that Turing hoped to build was called the Automatic Computing Engine, or ACE. It would be far more than just a chess-playing machine: if successful, ACE could solve any problem for which it received adequate programming. Turing relished the idea of writing programs, which he referred to as "instruction tables." It was the type of challenge he loved. "Instruction tables will have to be made

Computer scientists working on the Automatic Computing Engine in 1950. *(Courtesy of AP Images)*

up by mathematicians with computing experience and perhaps a certain puzzle-solving ability," he wrote. "There will probably be a good deal of work of this kind to be done, for every known process has got to be translated into instruction table form at some stage."

With the Delilah project, Turing had helped to physically construct the device, but now he would leave that job to the National Physics Laboratory engineers. He was more interested in devising the operational commands for the electronic brain.

As always, Alan Turing created headaches for his employers. During the war, his unorthodox behavior offended the sensibilities of professional officers. At NPL, he would chafe under the authority of his supervisor, a man named J. R. Womersley. Although Womersley came from a technical background, he was in actuality a government bureaucrat. He possessed the social skills Turing lacked, but was no match for the Turing intellect. As superintendent of NPL's mathematics division, he was responsible for overseeing the ACE project and Turing resented what he perceived as Womersley's interference in the project. Friction between the two men soon developed.

Turing was working in an environment far different from the one he had during the war. At Bletchley Park, the urgency of a possible German invasion meant that the codebreakers would receive every resource they needed. But in postwar Britain, government leaders focused on helping the nation recover economically. They concentrated on long-neglected social programs, placing limits on funding for scientific endeavors such as ACE. The result was slower progress than Turing would have preferred.

Even worse from Turing's point of view, he could not work in isolation at NPL and was required to perform tasks he considered to be a waste of time, such as attending meetings and filling out paperwork. He was forced to get approval before allotting resources to new ideas and had to wait while his requests were considered. It was the type of atmosphere that Alan Turing despised, and to him J. R. Womersley embodied. Womersley, for his part, regarded Turing as a preening egotist who made unreasonable requests.

Despite his frustrations at work, there were some positive developments in Turing's life during the mid-1940s. He achieved some success at competitive running. He had previously considered running to be a way to exercise and clear his mind. But in 1946, he began competing in amateur

Turing takes second place in a three-mile race. *(Courtesy of King's College Library, Cambridge)*

events. He specialized in long-distance races and frequently he finished at the front of the pack. In August, he completed the twenty-six miles of a marathon in a respectable two hours and forty-six minutes, good enough to earn him a fifth-place finish. "The last year or two I have taken to running rather a lot," he told a friend. "This is a form of compensation for not having been good at games at school."

In addition to his athletic accomplishments, Turing was receiving wider attention for his work. The British people still did not know of his codebreaking achievements during World War II, but his work at NPL was no secret. In the United States, a thirty-ton behemoth known as ENIAC became the world's first fully functional computer and the public skepticism about "thinking machines" was replaced with keen interest. Newspaper reporters quizzed Turing about potential uses for the ACE machine, once it was completed. Before long, he was receiving invitations to radio talk shows to discuss his views on computers and artificial intelligence. Although not quite a household name, Alan Turing was becoming recognized as a leader in the exciting new field of computer science. However, he was already moving in a different direction.

six

Mathematical Biology

A t the National Physics Laboratory, Alan Turing was growing ever more impatient with bureaucratic indecision and delays. Two years had passed since he had joined NPL and the ACE computer was still far from becoming a reality. As the engineers struggled to overcome the machine's physical challenges, Turing continued writing instruction tables—or programs, as they came to be called— for it. In essence, he was laying the groundwork for future generations of computer programmers.

As Turing's programs grew in size and scope, so too did his expectations for the machine's capabilities. He spoke of computers that could store millions of bits of information, and he disparagingly compared the memory capacity of the ACE with that of a minnow. Clearly, Turing's fertile mind was sprinting well ahead of the technical realities of 1947. He was publicly discussing advances in computer science that NPL had no hope of delivering in the near future. The situation understandably embarrassed NPL's administrators, who considered Turing arrogant and troublesome. In the fall of 1947, they proposed that Turing take a one-year sabbatical at King's College, his old academic home, to develop his ideas further.

Once back at King's, Turing drifted away from the theoretical work of computer programming and took a renewed interest in the physical sciences. The subject of his latest research was the human brain. Now more than ever, he desperately wanted to understand how that mysterious organ produced thought. Unfortunately, modern science could not yet explain the process to his satisfaction. As his sabbatical drew to a close, Turing was faced with the unpleasant prospect of returning to the National Physics Laboratory. The ACE project had continued to stagnate during his absence, and he saw no reason to expect any progress in the near future.

Meanwhile, engineers at the University of Manchester in northern England were advancing rapidly with their computer, the Manchester Mark I. In May 1948, the university offered Turing a position on that project. According to the terms of his sabbatical, Turing was supposed to return to the NPL staff for a period of at least two years. After some thought, he decided to break that promise. The Manchester Mark I was nearing completion, and it was simply too tempting an opportunity for him to pass up.

As compensation to the NPL, Turing produced a paper called "Intelligent Machinery," which summarized everything he had learned about artificial intelligence. NPL administrators, unimpressed with the document, declined to publish it. Turing set the paper aside and did not seek its publication elsewhere. However, many artificial intelligence experts today view "Intelligent Machinery" as an important early work in their field.

In the paper, Turing compared a computer with the untrained mind of an infant. He explained that both machine and child require two forces—discipline and initiative—to learn and become intelligent. Children acquire discipline and initiative from their parents. Regarding computers, Turing said, "So far we have been considering only discipline." He was referring to the many instruction tables that he and others had written to date. Turing then offered an idea for instilling computers with the other key quality, initiative:

> This would probably take the form of programming the machine to do every kind of job that could be done, as a matter of principle, whether it were economical to do it by machine or not. Bit by bit one would be able to allow the machine to make more and more "choices" or "decisions." One would eventually find it possible to programme it so as to make its behaviour be the logical result of a comparatively small number of general principles. When these became sufficiently general, interference would no longer be necessary, and the machine would have "grown up."

In "Intelligent Machinery," Turing also touched on a concept that he would later refine and call the "imitation game." Others subsequently renamed it the Turing test. It attempted to determine when a computer had actually acquired intelligence. Turing argued that, in order for a machine to be considered intelligent, it must be capable of conversing with people flawlessly, as if it too were human. He fleshed out the idea in another landmark paper titled "Computing Machinery and Intelligence," which appeared in October 1950 in the journal *Mind*.

Turing based his test on a popular party game of the time, in which a man and a woman leave the room. An interrogator then sends questions to both people, and they write carefully chosen responses, which are intended to offer no clues about their gender. Based on the two sets of responses, the interrogator must figure out who is the man and who is the woman. Turing proposed substituting a computer for one of the human players, so that the interrogator must instead distinguish between person and machine. He suspected that, by the close of the twentieth century, computers would advance to the point that an interrogator would struggle to make the correct identification. (As of 2007, however, no computer had ever passed the Turing test.)

Turing's comparisons between mind and machine, plus his desire to understand the human brain's production of thought, took him deeper into the field of biology. It was the latest step in his lifelong intellectual exploration. During that marathon, he journeyed through mathematics, physics, cryptography, computers, and now biology. Along the way, he sought fundamental answers about the nature of life and human existence. Biology, it seemed, might help him answer some of the essential questions. He began with a phenomenon of nature that always intrigued him—Fibonacci numbers.

The Italian mathematician Leonardo Fibonacci wrote extensively in the thirteenth century about special sequences of numbers. In a Fibonacci series, each number is the sum of the two numbers that precede it (for example, 0, 1, 1, 2, 3, 5, 8, 13 . . .) Aside from its usefulness in mathematics, Fibonacci noticed that the pattern appears repeatedly in nature. For example, the reproduction of honeybees follows the Fibonacci sequence, as does the growth of certain plant

Leonardo Fibonacci

leaves, flowers, and fruits. The connection between mathematics and nature's apparent randomness fascinated Turing. From his youth, he had frequently paused during walks to study the growth of a daisy or the pattern on a pine cone.

A significant change in Turing's personal life accompanied the shift in his professional studies. In the summer of 1950, he purchased a modest house near Manchester. Previously, he

Many patterns in nature, such as the growth of a daisy, follow the Fibonacci sequence.

had always been content to live in apartments and boarding houses, but at age thirty-eight he decided to settle down in his own home. He befriended the young couple next door, sharing afternoon tea and occasionally even doing some babysitting for them. He also made halfhearted attempts at domestic life, such as growing a garden and installing a brick walkway. Household chores and hobbies could not keep his attention, however, and the new home soon looked like a cluttered college dorm room.

There was also a new person in Turing's life. In late 1951, he met a young man named Arnold Murray on the streets of Manchester. At just nineteen, Murray was half Turing's age. The friendly youth was accustomed to hardship, having grown up in a poor family during the lean years of World War II. When Turing met him, Murray was unemployed and emaciated. Feeling a combination of pity and sexual attraction, Turing offered to buy the downtrodden young man a meal at a nearby restaurant, and Murray gratefully accepted.

As they ate, Turing extended an invitation for Murray to stay in his home over the upcoming weekend. Murray accepted the invitation but when the weekend arrived, he did not show up. Turing was disappointed; he felt a strong connection with the pale, blue-eyed young man. He returned to Manchester the following week and found Murray again wandering the city streets. This time, they returned to Turing's house and began a sexual relationship. Turing was happy when he was with Murray. He felt a sense of closeness and understanding that he had not known since his friendship with Joan Clarke. While Murray, unlike Clarke, could not hope to grasp the ideas Turing frequently discussed, he still listened with rapt attention.

Trouble soon arose, though. After one of Murray's visits in January 1952, Turing discovered that several bills were missing from his wallet. Furious, he wrote a letter to Murray dissolving their friendship, but when Murray reappeared a few days later and insisted he had no knowledge of the missing money Turing believed him. The relationship resumed, but soon Murray was asking for small loans to pay off unexplained debts. Turing ignored his better judgment and gave Murray the money.

Meanwhile, Turing's work in biology progressed. The study of Fibonacci patterns in nature led him to a more basic question—how living things grow and develop into the shapes that are familiar to us. He wondered, for example, how the cells in a fish egg know to assemble themselves into fins, scales, and gills. How do leopards get their spots? What causes a nondescript clump of cells to grow into the complex shape of a human embryo? By the 1950s, the role of genes was becoming better understood. Genes contain the blueprints for an organism, but Turing wondered how the plans in those blueprints were carried out. The process is called morphogenesis, and very little investigation had been done into it before Turing took it up.

Turing and Morphogenesis

Morphogenesis, meaning "generation of form," refers to the manner in which cells grow and organize into the shapes of living organisms. It is a branch of developmental biology. At first glance, morphogenesis might appear to be an odd subject for Alan Turing to study. He had typically preferred the concrete world of numbers, as opposed to the seeming unpredictability of nature.

As usual, Turing approached biology in an unorthodox manner. He suspected there was more order to the natural world than could be seen on the surface. Specifically, he believed that mathematics helped determine the shape and appearance of living things. In 1952, he published a paper entitled "The Chemical Basis of Morphogenesis." It was an extremely scholarly and involved work, particularly for someone with no formal background in the natural sciences. "The full understanding of the paper requires a good knowledge of mathematics, some biology, and some elementary chemistry," Turing admitted in its introduction.

He proposed that various chemicals influence an organism's structure while it is still an embryo. These chemicals, which he called morphogens, interact with one another to form different patterns. Those patterns, in turn, affect how cells organize and grow. Turing referred to his hypothesis as chemical embryology. He used early computers to calculate the biological impact of different chemical interactions. With complex algorithms, he was able to reproduce patterns that routinely appear in nature, such as the dappling of color found on dairy cows.

Turing's theory has never been proved or disproved, but "The Chemical Basis of Morphogenesis" continues to attract the interest of developmental biologists. Turing wrote other papers on biology, but none were published until after his death. He also left behind a virtual blizzard of handwritten notes on the subject. Some of the ideas described in those notes are still not fully understood.

Turing enlisted many of his previous passions to attack the problem. As a child, he had dabbled in chemistry. Once again, he performed experiments to learn how various chemicals interact in nature. In the 1930s and 1940s, he had helped make computers a reality. Now, computers assisted him in his mathematical analysis. The Manchester University computer lab was operational, and Turing stayed up very late at night running programs that would help him unravel the mysteries of nature.

In early 1952, Turing returned home after one of those late nights to discover that his house had been broken into and ransacked. It was a horrible shock, but he was relieved to learn that few items of value had been taken. Given his recent experiences, Turing suspected that Arnold Murray had something to do with the burglary but he did not mention this suspicion when reporting to the police. Homosexuality was still a crime in England, and Turing did not wish to draw undue attention to his relationship with Murray. Instead, he wrote another letter to the young man, once again terminating their clandestine relationship. As before, Murray responded by paying a visit, but this time he did not claim ignorance.

Murray had his own theory regarding the break-in. He admitted that he had been boasting about his association with Alan Turing in the bars of Manchester. In particular, he had confided in a streetwise acquaintance named Harry. Harry had proposed that he and Murray burglarize the house while Turing was away, but Murray insisted that he had refused. He felt certain Harry had decided to go ahead with the job anyway.

Murray's revelation presented Turing with a dilemma. He wanted to pass along the tip about Harry to the police, but he knew that the investigators would ask him where he had obtained the information. Accordingly, he concocted an elaborate story that concealed his friendship with Murray. It was a mistake. Police detectives had already connected Harry to the robbery through fingerprints taken at Turing's home. When caught, Harry confessed to the crime and told the police about the illicit relationship between Turing and Arnold Murray.

The detectives were unsure how to proceed. Alan Turing was an esteemed scientist and a respected figure in the community who they did not want to accuse of homosexuality based on the word of a confessed criminal. When Turing walked into the police station, offering his strange tale, the detectives had all the evidence they needed. He may have been a person of importance, as well as the victim of a crime, but apparently Alan Turing was guilty of breaking a different law. The investigation shifted from robbery to what was called "gross indecency" by British law of the time. A man found guilty of homosexual activity could be sentenced to two years in prison.

Turing was forthright when asked about his sexual identity. He had initially hoped to keep his secret hidden, but when interrogated he refused to deny his true nature. He admitted to having an affair with Arnold Murray and provided the detectives with a five-page statement candidly describing the details of that affair. The officers handling Turing's case admired his honesty but could not overlook his offense. Criminal charges would be filed against him. The only question that remained was the severity of his punishment.

seven

Poison Apple

In 1885, Britain's Parliament passed the Criminal Law Amendment Act, which was intended to institute a sweeping social reform of sexual activity. Among other provisions, it outlawed brothels and established the minimum age of sexual consent at sixteen. Although the primary goal was to protect women and children from sexual exploitation, the law also criminalized homosexual acts between males. (At the time, female homosexuality was considered too rare to address.)

Parliament changed the law in 1967 to permit private homosexual acts between consenting adults, but that revision was still fifteen years away at the time of Alan Turing's arrest. In March 1952, he pleaded guilty to gross indecency. He initially entertained the notion of a not-guilty plea, but his older brother John, who was an attorney, persuaded him otherwise. A trial would only result in additional publicity and a near certain verdict of guilty. The entire matter stunned John Turing, who had no idea his younger brother was gay.

Despite Alan Turing's guilty plea, the judge sensed no remorse—Turing felt he had done nothing wrong. Such an attitude usually translated into a harsher sentence. Yet Turing was an educated man, the recipient of an important British medal, and a first-time offender. Prison seemed inappropriate for him. The defense attorney, Mr. G. Lind-Smith, urged lenience and emphasized Turing's academic contributions. "He is entirely absorbed in his work," Lind-Smith asserted, "and it would be a loss if a man of his ability—which is no ordinary ability—were not able to carry on with it. The public would lose the benefit of the research work he is doing. There is treatment which could be given him. I ask you to think that the public interest would not be well served if this man is taken away from the very important work he is doing."

The treatment that Lind-Smith referred to was an experimental drug therapy that involved regular injections of estrogen, the female sex hormone, in an attempt to stifle the male libido. While the treatment's overall effectiveness was dubious, its side effects were known and included temporary impotency and the growth of breasts. Regardless, when the judge gave Turing a choice between prison time and a year of hormonal therapy plus probation, he chose the latter.

He was pleased that the treatments did not affect his thought processes, allowing him to continue his experiments in biology. In social settings, Turing tended to trivialize his brush with the law, lightheartedly recounting his court appearances to friends. No matter how much he joked, however, his conviction carried serious consequences. The most important of these was the loss of his government security clearance. Since the end of World War II, Turing had served as a cryptography consultant to the British intelligence community. That arrangement would no longer be possible.

The depth of his intelligence work during the postwar period is unknown, but shortly after the trial Turing was informed that his services were no longer needed. Official policy was that homosexuals could not be trusted with state secrets. Even if Turing's sexual orientation had not alarmed the spy agencies, his sudden interest in foreign travel almost certainly would have. Turing began to vacation in more culturally tolerant European nations, far from the reach of Britain's draconian anti-homosexuality statute.

The terms of Turing's plea agreement did not require him to seek psychiatric treatment, but in the fall of 1952 he took that step himself. He told a friend that he hoped the psychiatrist would put him in "a more resigned frame of mind" about his circumstances. His visits with therapist Franz Greenbaum bore little resemblance to the traditional doctor-patient relationship. Greenbaum knew of Turing's interest in the human mind, as well as his mathematic and scientific prowess. They spoke to each other as equals, analyzing Turing's psyche together. The sessions did not revolve around Turing's sexuality but attempted to uncover the root of his unhappiness.

Greenbaum's techniques, which included dream interpretation, often pointed to Turing's mother. Sara Turing was always concerned with appearances, and in that regard her younger son usually let her down. She had habitually fussed over his frayed clothes and haphazard grooming and chided him about his inclination toward solitude, saying that he needed more friends. She was also a deeply religious person, while her younger son was not and tired of her constantly foisting her beliefs upon him.

Ironically, the connection between mother and son grew stronger as Alan Turing aged. When his father died in 1947, she came closer to accepting her son for who he was. She also took pride in his achievements. His arrest no doubt caused her embarrassment, but she never complained to him about it, even when the details appeared in the newspapers. Sara Turing also took a small part in her son's biology research, gathering wildflower specimens for him. The woman who began as his harshest critic would ultimately become his greatest supporter.

The year 1953 brought many positive developments. In April, his probationary period ended, and so did the hormone treatments. A month later, Manchester University extended his employment for at least five more years. Turing celebrated these events with a summer trip to Paris and Greece.

Upon returning, he resumed the experiments that bubbled along in various rooms of his house. He also continued writing. Turing authored an essay on computerized chess that was published later in the year. In early 1954, he wrote a mathematical article for the popular journal *Science News* that explained to average readers the concept of solvable versus unsolvable problems. This was a new twist for Turing. His previous writings were academic papers aimed at a highly educated audience, his more recent works attempted to share his ideas with the public.

In 1953, Turing celebrated his extended tenure at Manchester University with a trip to Paris. *(Library of Congress)*

Turing even began to try his hand at creative writing, penning a short story about a studious gay man. The tale obviously drew on Turing's personal experiences, though the story line did not follow the actual events of his life. Turing's foray into fiction writing accompanied a newfound appreciation for literature and may have been influenced by his growing friendship with the British author and literary critic Philip Nicholas Furbank. It was also evidence that the horizons of his remarkable mental life were further expanding beyond the familiar territory of mathematics, science, and logic.

But the life of Alan Turing and his remarkable mind ended abruptly on June 7, 1954. He was alone. The following day his housekeeper discovered his body, lying peacefully on his bed. A partially eaten apple sat on the nightstand beside him, and froth clung to the corners of his mouth.

An autopsy revealed the cause of death as cyanide poisoning, and the coroner ruled it a suicide. Apparently, Turing had chosen to end his life by reenacting a scene from his favorite movie, *Snow White and the Seven Dwarfs*, in which the heroine bites into a poisoned apple. Since first seeing the Walt Disney animated epic in 1937, Turing had often jokingly invoked the witch's chant in conversation: "Dip the apple in the brew,/Let the sleeping death seep through."

Turing's body was cremated on June 12, 1954, in accordance with his wishes. He was less than two weeks away from turning forty-two.

In the wake of Alan Turing's death, his shocked family and friends struggled for an explanation as to why he might have taken his own life. While it was true that very few people, if anyone, really understood Turing, there seemed to be little reason for him to commit suicide. His

The witch offers Snow White a poisoned apple in this scene from Turing's favorite movie, *Snow White and the Seven Dwarfs*. *(Courtesy of Walt Disney Pictures/ZUMA Press)*

legal troubles were over, his job was secure, and he had no financial worries. He was in good health and could look forward to many productive years. His relationship with his mother was better than ever and he communicated regularly with the handful of friends he had accumulated over his lifetime. He was even beginning to show interest in matters that previously held no appeal for him. If any emotional pressures were weighing on him at the time, he kept them to himself. No suicide note was ever found.

In addition to having no apparent reason to kill himself, Turing gave no indication that he was contemplating suicide.

His behavior in the days and weeks leading up to his death seemed typical for him. His office at Manchester University was a clutter of open files and unfinished programs and he had scheduled his usual late-night sessions in the computer lab for the week following June 7. Days before his death he invited his next-door neighbors over for dinner. The young family was planning to move, and Turing spoke cheerfully of visiting them in their new home. Tickets for an upcoming play sat on his desk, as did professional correspondence that he had not yet had a chance to mail.

To Sara Turing, all of this added up to one thing: the official explanation of her son's death was wrong. He had not committed suicide, she insisted, but rather had died in a tragic accident. Sara Turing pointed out, correctly, that he frequently used cyanide and other dangerous chemicals in his scientific experiments. On at least one occasion she had cautioned him to be careful, but he shrugged off her warnings. Following his death, several jars containing cyanide mixtures were found in his house. Sara Turing speculated that her son had been working with one of these and carelessly got some of the solution on his hands. It was well known that Turing had a habit of eating an apple before going to sleep. In this instance, Sara Turing claimed, he must have transferred some of the poison from his hands to the apple and unknowingly ingested it.

Because the coroner did not test the apple for traces of cyanide, there was no way to definitively prove or disprove Mrs. Turing's theory. Her view was certainly plausible—and some observers who accepted the official explanation suggested that Turing had wanted it that way. Because he had not wished to cause his mother undue emotional pain, they claimed, he had deliberately left no clues pointing to his suicide and had carefully chosen a method that would allow her to believe his death had been accidental.

Some who believe Turing did kill himself point out that he had made passing comments about suicide at various points in his life. In 1937, while at Princeton, Turing had even told a friend that he had devised a scheme for taking one's life. The plan included an apple attached to some electrical wiring. However, such talk hardly constitutes evidence of an actual suicide more than a decade and a half later. Similarly, definitive conclusions cannot be drawn from two incidents that occurred in 1954, although those incidents might be interpreted as suggestive of Turing's sense of an impending end. Four months before his death, he updated his last will and testament, and in May, just weeks before his body was found, he emerged pale and visibly shaken from a half-hour session with a boardwalk fortune-teller. The friends with him on the Sunday excursion to the seashore reported that Turing did not say another word for the rest of the day.

Today, the uncertainty surrounding Alan Turing's death lingers. While it is widely accepted that Turing died by his own hand, the possibility of accidental poisoning cannot be ruled out. After the details of Turing's cryptanalytic achievements became known several historians suggested a third possibility: murder. Again, the case for murder is not supported by solid evidence but is based on conjecture.

At Bletchley Park, Turing was at the center of many highly sensitive British military programs; during his 1942 visit to the United States, he also became privy to American military secrets. The nature of his postwar work for the British secret service remains a mystery, but it is reasonable to assume that he was involved in highly classified Cold War projects. After the revelation of Turing's homosexuality in 1952, the British government severed all connections with him, but it is unknown whether he continued to be viewed as a security risk.

Months earlier, a Soviet spy ring had been uncovered at the University of Cambridge. Two members of that ring, Guy Burgess and Donald Maclean, defected to the Soviet Union in 1951. Both men were intellectuals, and Burgess was a homosexual. Turing's frequent visits to other countries, some of which rested within the sphere of Soviet influence, may have aroused suspicion among British intelligence officers.

Some historians have wondered whether Turing was killed to prevent the many important secrets he knew from falling into the hands of the Soviet Union. It is possible that this theory, like the others, will never be proved or disproved. Like certain mathematical problems, the mystery of Alan Turing's death might never be solved.

eight
Alan Turing's Legacy

In May 1997, the IBM supercomputer Deep Blue defeated chess champion Garry Kasparov in a six-game tournament. It was the first time that an international grandmaster lost to a computer in match play. Deep Blue's 256 parallel processors enabled it to calculate more than one-hundred million chess positions per second. After the match, Kasparov acknowledged that the computer's unrelenting assault gradually wore him down mentally.

Half a century earlier, Alan Turing had sat in his office at the National Physics Laboratory and written out the fundamental logic that would govern Deep Blue's programming—and all computer programs, for that matter. At a time when the handful of computers in existence still depended on vacuum tubes and punch cards to perform the most elementary of tasks, Turing predicted that computers would eventually challenge the human mind. He considered the game of chess

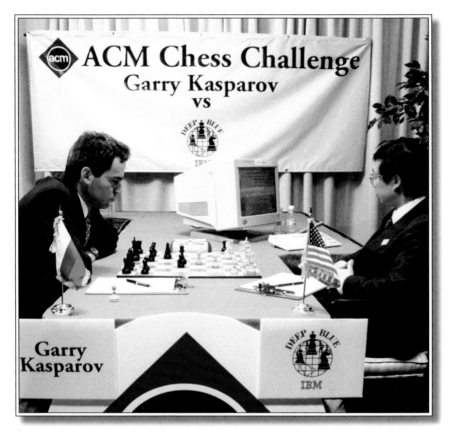

Garry Kasparov (left) plays a chess match against the IBM supercomputer Deep Blue in 1997. *(Courtesy of AP Images/George Widman)*

an ideal arena for demonstrating their immense processing capacity. The success of Deep Blue against Kasparov, a man widely regarded as one of the greatest chess players ever, was a fitting symbol of Alan Turing's legacy.

Through computers, Turing did not hope to defeat the human mind, but rather to understand it. His desire to know the basis of thought was the defining element of his career. Unlike many great scholars, Turing refused to confine himself to a single field of study. Historians cannot narrowly label him as a mathematician, a physicist, a cryptographer, a computer scientist, or a biologist. Instead, he was all of these. Turing delved into each discipline, eagerly searching for the answers he wanted. Before moving on, he typically left behind a new discovery or revelation that startled the field's experts. With his unconventional approach, he was able to interpret data in ways they could not.

As a child, Alan Turing displayed behavior that today might lead to the diagnosis of a mild form of autism. An obsession with numbers and patterns, a lack of social skills, and a difficulty communicating with others are all characteristics now associated with that disorder. Later in life, his ability to relate to others improved slightly, but Turing never lost his fixation with repetitive sequences or his penchant to work alone. To his parents and teachers, he always seemed withdrawn and preoccupied. Despite their best efforts, they could never enter his remote world of logic and equations. Slowly, they stopped trying to interfere and permitted him to develop in his own unique way.

When he reached adulthood, Turing's intellect fully blossomed, and he began making the groundbreaking contributions for which he is known today. The first of these, the universal Turing machine, came to him at the age of twenty-three. He used the theoretical Turing machine to prove the existence of unsolvable problems in mathematics. While other mathematicians were reaching the same conclusion via traditional methods, Turing's proof was far more direct and elegant. The Turing machine, however, did more than help answer an important mathematical question. It ushered in the age of computer science. Turing showed the world the true potential of mechanical devices, and his abstract machine served as a blueprint for the first working computers. The universal Turing machine remains a key concept in computer science today.

It is difficult to exaggerate the importance of Alan Turing's contributions to his country during World War II. During much of 1940 and 1941, Britain faced the Nazi onslaught virtually alone. Continental Europe had fallen, and the United States had yet to enter the conflict. American supplies, which had to be shipped across the Atlantic Ocean, provided the island nation a thin lifeline. Hitler realized that Britain could not survive without the American aid, and German U-boats fought tenaciously to sever the Atlantic supply line. If not for Alan Turing and his Bletchley Park colleagues, the Germans may have succeeded.

The dedication and bravery of the British and American sailors who grappled with the U-boats on the vast Atlantic battlefield must not be overlooked. However, without the crucial intelligence provided by Bletchley Park, their victory would certainly have come at a much higher cost, and possibly not at all. In Hut 8, Turing worked at the heart of the espionage war against the German navy. His cunning innovations with the Polish bombes were essential to cracking the Enigma cipher. By decrypting German messages, the Allies were able to neutralize the U-boat threat and keep the shipping lanes open. Great Britain survived, and in 1944, it served as a launching platform for the invasion of occupied Europe and the eventual defeat of Nazi Germany.

Following the war, Turing returned to the emerging field of computer science and pioneered computer programming. Ultimately, he found that the technology of the day could not keep pace with his grand plans to simulate human thought and approached the problem from a new direction. He turned to biology, examining the chemical nature of organisms. Although he made some significant discoveries in developmental biology, it was his least successful endeavor. He was still struggling to uncover the secrets of the human brain when he died in 1954.

Turing's death drew few headlines in Britain. In the years immediately following World War II, he obtained a small degree of celebrity as one of the nation's foremost computer experts. But by the 1950s, he was fading into obscurity. Elsewhere in the world he had never even been known, so his death went completely unnoticed.

In 1959, Sara Turing published a brief biography of her son. She was intent on setting the record straight and securing his rightful place in history. The book contained valuable information about Alan's early life, but Mrs. Turing was unable to describe adequately his activities as an adult. Much of Turing's technical work was beyond her grasp—and in the case of his Bletchley Park cryptanalysis, was still classified. She also carefully avoided what she considered to be the more embarrassing details of his personal life.

Only in the 1970s did the British codebreakers' invaluable wartime efforts come to public light. Their cryptanalytic methods obsolete, the Bletchley Park veterans were at last free to tell their story. Several books heralded the secret war that the nation's best mathematicians had waged against Nazi Germany. Alan Turing received credit for his part in the struggle, but his entire story was not told until 1983, when the first comprehensive Turing biography was published. Recognition of Alan Turing as a war hero and as the father of computer science has steadily grown since that time.

Each year, the Association for Computing Machinery presents the A. M. Turing Award to an individual who has made an outstanding contribution to computer science. The honor is often described as the Nobel Prize of computing, and carries a $100,000 cash award. Several other awards and scholarships also bear Turing's name and many universities have named computer labs after him. In 2004, the University of Manchester opened the Alan Turing Institute, a prestigious research center for math, science, and technology. A city street in Manchester is named Alan Turing Way, and a bronze statue of him adorns a nearby park. Another statue graces the campus of the University of Surrey in Guildford. In London, Turing's birthplace is designated a national landmark.

Alan Turing never cared much about public accolades, but these honors confirm the world's belated recognition of his work. Turing was among the first to grasp the limitless possibilities of mechanical computation, and it took years—sometimes even decades—of technological advances before his visionary ideas could begin to be translated into reality. Today, of course, the use of computers in everyday life is ubiquitous. But during Turing's time, the early computers were encumbered by inefficient and unreliable vacuum tubes, which were only beginning to be replaced by the transistor. In the 1960s, integrated circuits replaced individual transistors, and by the 1970s, integrated circuit technology gave rise to the microprocessor. Today's microprocessors can contain more than 40 million tiny transistors. Computer technology is advancing at an exponential rate; the number of transistors possible to mount on a single integrated circuit (an indication of the speed of a microprocessor) doubles roughly every two years, a phenomenon known as Moore's Law. Computers have become smaller, faster, and more powerful than could possibly have been imagined sixty years ago, and there is no indication the trend will slow.

Despite the astonishing evolution of hardware and software, computers are still not capable of independent thought.

The Turing Test Today

Alan Turing argued that computers cannot be deemed intelligent until they are capable of successfully engaging in human conversation. According to the rules of his test, a human judge must carry out a written discussion with two anonymous subjects, one of which is a computer. If the judge cannot distinguish between the human and the computer based on their responses, then the computer has succeeded. Turing predicted that by the year 2000, computers would be capable of fooling human judges roughly one-third of the time.

Since 1990, the Loebner Prize for artificial intelligence has offered $100,000 to the individual or team who develops the first computer to provide responses that are indistinguishable from human responses. To date, the prize has not been awarded. Each year, a new set of contestants make the attempt, but the judges are always able to discern human from machine. Instead, a $2,000 consolation prize is given to the entrant whose computer comes closest to appearing human.

In recent years, some artificial intelligence experts have questioned the value of the Turing test. They say the test, in addition to being impossibly difficult, proves nothing about the presence or lack of intelligence in computers. As evidence, they cite the fact that most Loebner Prize contestants enter chatterbox programs of the kind sometimes found in Internet chat rooms. Chatterboxes simply scan for keywords and then select a canned response from a database. A computer running a chatterbox program has no comprehension of the discussion in which it is participating.

Critics of the Turing test believe there must be a better way to measure computer intelligence. One alternative they have suggested is RoboCup—an international project that seeks to field a team of soccer-playing robots. RoboCup's ultimate goal is to compete and win against human soccer teams by the year 2050. Each year, the project's members hold a competition to demonstrate their progress.

With his test, Alan Turing set the stage for a grand philosophical debate about artificial intelligence (AI). Proponents of "strong AI" believe that computers are indeed capable of thought and self-awareness, while "weak AI" advocates claim that computers will never be anything more than mindless followers of instructions. The debate is sure to rage on as computers become even more powerful and sophisticated.

In this sense, Alan Turing's "electronic brain" has yet to be invented.

Today's scientists do have a better understanding of how human brains think. If Turing were alive and conducting research today, he would no doubt be considered a "cognitive scientist." The field of cognitive science emerged in the mid-1970s, when it was realized that a proper study of the human mind requires a multifaceted approach. Cognitive science draws on biology, psychology, philosophy, physics, and computer science, as well as other disciplines, to understand the complex functioning of the human mind. Topics of study include memory, language, attention, and learning. One can only imagine the advances Turing would have made in these areas had he lived a normal lifespan.

In his era, Alan Turing's sexual orientation and peculiar habits made him something of a social outcast. It did not seem to bother him; he was always more concerned with the details of his work than with making friends or winning admiration. Whether his detachment from society ultimately played a role in his death will never be known. The only thing that can be said with any certainty is that Alan Turing was a brilliant individual who, in his own way, made remarkable contributions to the pool of human knowledge.

Turing once noted that a person spends roughly the first two decades of life learning the discoveries of those who came before him. Afterward, Turing said, "he may then perhaps do a little research of his own and make a very few discoveries which are passed on to other men." It is a modest but fitting description of Alan Turing's own life.

A bronze statue of Turing in a Manchester park, close to Alan Turing Way *(Courtesy of Andy Marshall/Alamy)*

Timeline

1912   Born on June 23 in England.

1930   Receives a scholarship to King's College, Cambridge.

1936   Uses a theoretical computer, know as the Turing machine, to prove that unsolvable mathematical problems do exist; in September, travels to the United States and begins studies at Princeton University.

1938   Returns to Britain and begins working as a codebreaker for the Government Code and Cypher School.

1939   Spends the next three years at Bletchley Park cracking the German navy's highly advanced Enigma cipher.

1941   Proposes marriage to co-worker Joan Clarke, but the engagement is short lived; Turing accepts the fact that he is a homosexual.

1942   Travels to Washington, D.C., to help United States cryptanalysts set up their codebreaking program.

1943   Sails back to Britain and commences work on a voice-encryption system, which is

code-named Delilah; transfers from Bletchley
Park to Hanslope Park.

1945   Accepts employment at the National
Physics Laboratory, where he joins a team that
is trying to build a prototype computer called
the Automatic Computing Engine (ACE);
begins pioneering work in the field of computer
programming.

1947   Returns to King's College for a one-year
sabbatical; turns his attention from computers
to the fundamental question of how humans
produce thought.

1948   Takes a job at the University of Manchester,
where a computer called the Manchester Mark
I is ready to become operational; uses
the computer lab at Manchester to do
groundbreaking work in the field of
developmental biology.

1951   Becomes sexually involved with a young man
named Arnold Murray.

1952   Charged with gross indecency after police learn
of his relationship with Murray; pleads guilty
and submits to an experimental drug therapy.

1954   Alan Turing dies on June 7; his death is
officially ruled a suicide.

Sources

CHAPTER ONE: Early Discoveries

p. 18, "Though he had been loved . . ." Andrew Hodges, *Alan Turing: The Enigma* (New York: Simon & Schuster, 1983), 19–20.

p. 19, "[Einstein] has now got to . . ." Ibid., 34.

p. 23, "As regards the question . . ." Ibid., 64.

CHAPTER TWO: Universal Turing Machine

p. 24, "Its programme is principally . . . " Hodges, *Alan Turing*, 71.

p. 32, "The graduate students . . ." Ibid., 119.

p. 32, "Description of travel . . ." Ibid.

CHAPTER THREE: Unraveling the Enigma

p. 47-48, "Dear Prime Minister, . . ." B. Jack Copeland, ed., *The Essential Turing: Seminal Writings in Computing, Logic, Philosophy, Artificial Intelligence, and Artificial Life plus the Secrets of Enigma* (New York: Oxford University Press, 2004), 338.

CHAPTER FIVE: Building a Brain

p. 64, "A great positive reason . . ." Copeland, *The Essential Turing*, 420.

p. 70-71, "Instruction tables will . . ." Hodges, *Alan Turing*, 326.

p. 73, "The last year or two . . ." Ibid., 369.

CHAPTER SIX: Mathematical Biology

p. 76, "So far we have been . . ." Copeland, *The Essential Turing*, 429.

p. 76, "This would probably take . . ." Ibid., 429-430.

p. 81, "The full understanding . . ." Ibid., 519.

CHAPTER SEVEN: Poison Apple

p. 86, "He is entirely absorbed . . ." Hodges, *Alan Turing*: The Enigma, 472.

p. 87, "a more resigned . . ." Ibid., 481.

CHAPTER EIGHT: Alan Turing's Legacy

p. 103, "he may then perhaps . . ." Copeland, *The Essential Turing*, 431.

Bibliography

Copeland, Jack B., ed. *Alan Turing's Automatic Computing Engine: The Master Codebreaker's Struggle to Build the Modern Computer.* New York: Oxford University Press, 2005.

_____. *The Essential Turing*: Seminal Writings in Computing, Logic, Philosophy, Artificial Intelligence, and Artificial Life plus the Secrets of Enigma. New York: Oxford University Press, 2004.

Hinsley, F. H., and Alan Stripp, eds. *Codebreakers: The Inside Story of Bletchley Park.* New York: Oxford University Press, 2001.

Hodges, Andrew. *Alan Turing: The Enigma.* New York: Simon & Schuster, 1983.

Leavitt, David. *The Man Who Knew Too Much: Alan Turing and the Invention of the Computer.* New York: W. W. Norton & Co., 2005.

Millican, Peter, and Andy Clark, eds. *Machines and Thought: The Legacy of Alan Turing, Volume I.* New York: Oxford University Press, 1996.

Strathern, Paul. *Turing and the Computer: The Big Idea.* New York: Random House, 1997.

Teuscher, Christof, ed. *Alan Turing: Life and Legacy of a Great Thinker.* New York: Springer, 2003.

Web sites

http://www.turingarchive.org/
A digital archive of Alan Turing's personal papers and photographs.

http://www.turing.org.uk/turing/
A fact-filled site maintained by Andrew Hodges, author of *Alan Turing: The Enigma*.

http://www.nationalcodescentre.org/
The official Web site of Bletchley Park, which is now a national museum dedicated to the British codebreakers.

http://enigmaco.de/index-enigma.html
An online simulator of the Enigma encryption machine.

http://www.chessgames.com/perl/chessgame?gid=1356927
A re-creation of what was effectively the first chess game between man and machine—the 1952 contest during which Alick Glennie faced Alan Turing's chess program.

http://www.turinghub.com/
Visitors to the Turing Hub can participate in an actual Turing test, deciding after a five-minute chat whether they were talking with a computer or a human.

http://www.loebner.net/Prizef/loebner-prize.html
Home page of the Loebner Prize, offered to the developers of the first computer program that passes the Turing test.

Index

Babbage, Charles, 27, *27*

Bayley, Donald, 57-58

Brewster, Edwin Tenney, 17

Burgess, Guy, 94

Champernowne, David, 24

Church, Alonzo, 31-32

Churchill, Winston, 47-48,
  48, 58

Clarke, Joan, 49, 55, 80

Disney, Walt, 90

Einstein, Albert, 18-19,
  20, 30

Fibonacci, Leonardo, 77, *78*

Furbank, Philip Nicholas, 90

Gandy, Robin, 56-57

Glennie, Alick, 67

Greenbaum, Franz, 87

Hilbert, David, 29, *30*

Hitler, Adolf, 25, *26*, 50, 58,
  98

Kasparov, Garry, 95-96, *96*

Lind-Smith, G., 86

Maclean, Donald, 94

Morcom, Christopher, 20-23

Murray, Arnold, 79-81, 83-84

Newton, Isaac, 19

Stoney, George Johnstone, 54

Turing, Alan, *12*, *16*, *21*, *31*,
  72, *103*
  Arrested for affair with
    Arnold Murray, 84
  Birth, 15
  Death, 90
  Death of father, 88
  Develops Automated
    Computing Engine, 70
  Develops theory for
    Turing Machine, 28-29
  Goes to work at
    Government Code and
    Cypher School, 37

Goes to work at National
 Physics Laboratory, 62
Goes to work at University
 of Manchester, 75
Honored with order of
 the British Empire, 61
Travels to U.S. to work as
 codebreaker, 50
Works,
  "Computing Machinery
   and Intelligence," 76
  Intelligent Machinery,"
   75-76
  "On Computable
   Numbers with an
   Application to the
   Entscheidungs
   Problem," 30
  "The Chemical Basis of
   Morphogenesis," 81-82

Turing, Ethel Sara Stoney
 (mother), *14*, 15, 17-18, 20,
 24, 26, 32, 87-88, 91-93, 99
Turing, John (brother), 15,
 20, 85-86
Turing, Julius (father), *15*,
 15, 17, 20, 26, 88

Von Neumann, John, 66

Womersley, J. R., 71-72